"My friend Brennan's message is timeless, and it comes to us with an authority you can feel. Read Brennan's story, his *Souvenirs of Solitude*, and enter more deeply into the story of Jesus."

—DR. LARRY CRABB, author and speaker;
founder/director, NewWay Ministries

"Once again, Brennan Manning's mind shows itself to be well-acquainted with the voice of God, drenched in real encounters with our personal God of Scripture, and fully persuaded that God loves us relentlessly."

—JAN JOHNSON, author of *Invitation to the Jesus Life*

"A moving account of one man's intimate encounters with God in solitude. Read it and be inspired to deepen your own journey of intimacy with God."

—RUTH HALEY BARTON, president, Transforming Center;
author of *Invitation to Solitude and Silence*

"Solitude is more than space and time. In this fine volume, Brennan Manning shows us the richness and potentiality of solitude in a series of warm, engaging reflections on spiritual living. This exploration is a grace and a gift. Enjoyable and provocative."

—EMILIE GRIFFIN, author of *Doors into Prayer: An Invitation*

"A gift from one of America's favorite spiritual authors. Reading these meditations allows us to be present with the author as he is present with God in the midst of the flow of his life. Read this book contemplatively and prepare to meet God in deep ways and places."

—DAVID G. BENNER, PhD, author of *Surrender to Love, The Gift of Being Yourself, and Desiring God's Will*

Souvenirs *of* Solitude

Finding Rest in Abba's Embrace

Brennan Manning

with Prayers by Sue Garmon

NAVPRESS®

NAVPRESS⬤.

NavPress is the publishing ministry of The Navigators, an international Christian organization and leader in personal spiritual development. NavPress is committed to helping people grow spiritually and enjoy lives of meaning and hope through personal and group resources that are biblically rooted, culturally relevant, and highly practical.

For a free catalog go to www.NavPress.com
or call 1.800.366.7788 in the United States or 1.800.839.4769 in Canada.

© 2009 by Brennan Manning

This book was originally released in 1979 by Dimension Books.

All rights reserved. No part of this publication may be reproduced in any form without written permission from NavPress, P.O. Box 35001, Colorado Springs, CO 80935. www.navpress.com

NAVPRESS and the NAVPRESS logo are registered trademarks of NavPress. Absence of * in connection with marks of NavPress or other parties does not indicate an absence of registration of those marks.

ISBN: 978-1-60006-867-6

Cover design by Arvid Wallen
Cover image by Shutterstock

Some of the anecdotal illustrations in this book are true to life and are included with the permission of the persons involved. All other illustrations are composites of real situations, and any resemblance to people living or dead is coincidental.

Unless otherwise identified, all Scripture quotations in this publication are taken from the *The Jerusalem Bible* (TJB), © 1966, 1967 and 1968 by Darton, Longman & Todd Ltd and Doubleday, a division of Random House. All Rights Reserved. Used by permission. Other versions used include the *Holy Bible, New International Version*˙ (NIV˙), Copyright © 1973, 1978, 1984 by International Bible Society, used by permission of Zondervan, all rights reserved.

Published in association with the literary agency of Alive Communications, Inc., 7680 Goddard St., Suite 200, Colorado Springs, CO 80920.

Library of Congress Cataloging-in-Publication Data
Manning, Brennan.
  Souvenirs of solitude : finding rest in Abba's embrace / Brennan
Manning ; with prayers by Sue Garmon. -- [2nd ed.].
      p. cm.
  Includes bibliographical references and index.
  ISBN 978-1-60006-867-6 (alk. paper)
  1. Solitude--Religious aspects--Christianity. 2. Spiritual life. 3.
Spiritual life--Catholic Church. I. Garmon, Sue. II. Title.
  BV4509.5.M27 2009
  248.4'7--dc22

                              2009014102

Printed in the United States of America

1 2 3 4 5 6 7 8 / 13 12 11 10 09

I am deeply grateful for my parents and to my parents. This book is a gift to my mom and dad, Amy and Emmett Manning, who taught me by their lives that it is more blessed to give than to receive.

We need to find God
and he cannot be found in noise and restlessness.

God is a friend of silence.
See how nature — trees, flowers, grass —
grow in silence.
See the stars, the moon, the sun,
how they move in silence.

Is not our mission
to give God to the poor?
Not a dead God, but a living, loving God.

The more we receive in silent prayer,
the more we can give in our active life.
We need silence
to be able to touch souls.

The essential thing is
not what we say,
but what God says
to us and through us.

All our words will be useless
unless they come from within.
   Words
         which do not give the Light of Christ
         increase the darkness.

                  — Mother Teresa of Calcutta

CONTENTS

Preface to the Second Edition

Souvenirs are remembrances, and as such they are not aware of today's date. This book is a series of remembrances that I recorded in the late 1970s. But as with all good remembrances, I believe they have a timeless quality and a value for readers today. Many of the themes I have been teaching since the late '60s and early '70s are captured in my fresh exhilaration in this book. Dominant among those themes is the astonishing, boundless love of God for us.

In the Hebrew tradition, to remember is to "make present." On the first night of Passover, there is a remarkable ritual in which the youngest child in a family goes to the father and asks, "Why is this night different from all other nights?" The father then proceeds to tell the story of the Exodus. In his telling—and in the child's hearing—the child becomes *B'nai B'rith*, or a son of the covenant. In the telling of the story, what happened thousands of years ago in the Exodus becomes a *present reality* to and in the young child.

In our Christian tradition, the Eucharist "makes present" the death of Christ for us. The Eucharist is more than just a fading, pleasant memory. In essence, Jesus said, "Do this in remembrance of me; and as you do this, I will become present to you in the bread and the cup."

Though less sacred and liturgical, the enclosed souvenirs of solitude are not just pleasant memories either. As you engage in them, I believe they will become present reality for you. While they contain many stories of my early life, I offer them as personal souvenirs in the hope they will become your own life-giving encounters with God today.

BRENNAN MANNING

New Orleans, Louisiana

Easter 2009

PREFACE TO THE FIRST EDITION

"*T*he man who prays will accomplish more in a year than another in a lifetime," wrote Louis Lallemant, eminent seventeenth-century French Jesuit.

Whatever effectiveness there is in my personal presence and ministry to others is anchored in the Eucharist and the thousands of hours of solitary prayer in caves, deserts, hermitages, airports, taxicabs, motel rooms, cells in private homes, rectories, and monasteries. Over the past two decades I have roamed this country and the world only to discover that I connect best with others when I connect with the core of myself. When I am able to disengage myself from others and allow the Lord to liberate me from an unhealthy dependence on people, I can exist more for them, listen more attentively, love more unselfishly, speak more compassionately, play more playfully, take myself less seriously, and become more aware that my face is bright with laughter in the midst of a game I thoroughly enjoy.

Silence and solitude are precious commodities in my life. My restless self finds peace only when I rest in God. How difficult it is to persuade others of the value of being alone with the Lord! Anne Morrow Lindbergh put it this way in *Gift from the Sea*:

As far as the search for solitude is concerned, we live in
a negative atmosphere as invisible, as all-pervasive, and

as enervating as high humidity in an August afternoon. The world today does not understand, in either man or woman, the need to be alone.

How inexplicable it seems. Anything else will be accepted as a better excuse. If one sets aside time for a business appointment, a trip to the hairdresser, a social engagement, or a shopping expedition, that time is accepted as inviolable. But if one says, I cannot come because that is my hour to be alone, one is considered rude, egotistical or strange. What a commentary on our civilization, when being alone is considered suspect; when one has to apologize for it, make excuses, hide the fact that one practices it — like a secret vice!

Actually these are among the most important times in one's life — when one is alone. Certain springs are tapped only when we are alone. The artist knows he must be alone to create; the writer, to work out his thoughts; the musician, to compose; the saint, to pray.[1]

Years ago I took the Myers-Briggs personality test to gain some insight and perspective on the junkyard I call my mind. I learned that I am an introvert-intuitive, feeler-perceiver type and that the most urgent need in my life is time alone. As a hungry man needs food and a thirsty man water, I need solitude — time to achieve a state of peace and recollection from which I can function and give to others what I was meant to in the personal plan of God for me.

Immediately guilt feelings arose. Is this need really hedging bets, evading responsibility, wasting time, an idle luxury? I found considerable comfort in the words of the Dutch Dominican Edward Schillebeeckx:

---

[1] Anne Morrow Lindbergh, *Gift from the Sea* (New York: Pantheon Books, 1955, 1975), 43–44.

Christianity, however involved it is in our everyday cares and tasks and all our secular activity, has a special sacral space set apart from secular developments and from culture, within which we grow in intimacy with God. Here we are simply together with God in Christ. Now, on a merely human level silence forms a part of discourse and social intercourse, though in and for itself it has no meaning; it has meaning only as a function of fellowship. It is necessary in order to make contact between men human and to keep it so — to humanize it. It is silence that makes speech personal. Without it, dialogue is impossible. But in a revealed religion, silence with God has a value in itself and for its own sake, just because God is God. Failure to recognize the value of mere being with God, as the Beloved, without doing anything, is to gouge the heart out of Christianity.[2]

These souvenirs of solitude are the love story of my walk with God. Revisiting the lost silences of the past, I remember and record the intimate moments when I allowed the Lord to lure me into the wilderness and speak to my heart. In chaste deserts, remote hermitages, and soaring 747s, the word of Jeremiah has become my own: "O Yahweh, you seduced me, and I let myself be seduced: you were too strong for me, and you triumphed" (20:7). If the Christian commitment were not an affair of the heart, I know I could not endure it. The real memorabilia of my life are these souvenirs of solitude, these moments of loving intercourse with the Bridegroom to whom I belong.

Solitude is not easy. In fact, Nikos Kazantzakis wrote, "Solitude can be fatal for the soul that does not burn with great passion." But the authenticity of my life project is at stake. Experience has taught

---

[2] Edward Schillebeeckx, O. P., "The Church and Mankind," trans. James A. Byrne, S. J., and Theodore L. Westow, in *The Church and Mankind: Dogma*, vol. 1 (Glen Rock, NJ: Paulist, 1964), 99.

me that if I am not in touch with the Christ of my own interiority, then I cannot touch others. If I am estranged from myself, I am likewise a stranger to others. Whatever loneliness, aridity, and desolation are involved (which may be considerable), time alone with God can be avoided only at the risk of grave peril.

In *Growth in the Spirit*, François Roustang said,

> The Spirit who gives meaning and value to all external courses of action and to all religious or secular acts must be experienced in the most remote solitudes. No one can escape this law. In their use of the words "heart," "soul," "deepest strata of the soul" or simply "depth," spiritual writers are not making a concession to pious jargon. They are trying to say in human language, following Christ, what eye cannot see and ear cannot hear. It is only when God gives them being, that they can find the Word of life externally, that they can hear his voice resound in the multiplicity of the things of this world.[3]

In these pages it is my pleasure to introduce the reader to the late Miss Sue Garmon of New Orleans, Louisiana. Many years ago, we were on a weekend retreat in Covington, Louisiana. Since that time, we shared our lives in prayer and collaborated in team ministry in various areas of her home state. The prayers at the end of each chapter are a window into the poetry of her spirit and reveal better than any words of mine the warmth and sensitivity, candor and honesty, love and longing of her tryst with the Bridegroom. It is with joy that I share her gift with you, and it is with honor that I call her my friend.

Asking a blessing on this book, I pray that these souvenirs jog your memory, put you in touch with the moments of God's

---

[3] François Roustang, S. J., *Growth in the Spirit*, trans. Kathleen Pond (New York: Sheed and Ward, 1966), 13.

loving intervention in your personal history, and make you more conscious of who you are, why you are here, and where you are going.

BRENNAN MANNING
Clearwater, Florida
September 1978

CHAPTER 1

THE SECOND SUMMONS

*F*or twenty-two years I have been trying to make my Christian identity the most important enterprise of my life. The old saw "Tell me how you distribute your time and your money, and I'll tell you who you are" gives me a guarded assurance that I have not been deceiving myself. Despite moments of weakness, obvious imperfections, moral relapses, and moments of selfishness, the overall tenor of my life has been fidelity to the truth as I understand it.

Jesus Christ is the truth for me. His Word influences my judgment, affects the decisions I make and the ones I refuse to make. His truth has helped me determine what is central in life and what is secondary, what is important and less important, what is crucial and what is marginal, fringe, peripheral. But is He real? Have I been "carrying coals to Newcastle"? Does rhetoric match reality? I have one life to live, and I want to live it to the hilt. Am I overcome by routine, perfunctory prayers, the ordinariness of life, by daily duties done over and over again? I trundle off to the desert to reexamine the direction of my life.

And the Lord summons me a second time. In the chastening solitude of the Pennsylvania hills, He extends a second invitation: "I want you to accept My Father's love." I answered, "But I know that. It's old hat. I've come up to this deserted place seeking new insight. I'm in a fit of fervor, red-hot, wide open. I'll listen to anything You have to say. Go ahead, Lord, dazzle me. Lay a new word on me. I know the old one."

And He answers, "That's just what you don't know—the old one. You have no idea of how much I love you. The moment you think you understand is the moment that you do not understand. I am God, not man. You travel the world telling others about Me—that I am a loving God. Your words are glib. How readily they roll off your tongue. My words are written in the blood of My only Son. The next time you preach of My life with such obnoxious familiarity, I may come and blow your prayer meeting apart. When you come at Me with your pedantic professionalism, I will expose you as a rank amateur. When you try to persuade others that you understand what you are talking about, I will reduce you to silence and hurl you flat on your face! You claim that you know that I love you. Then gird your loins like a man. Now I will question you, and you tell Me the answers.

"Do you know that every time you tell Me you love Me, I say thank you?

"When a fear-filled child comes to you in the darkness of a thunderstorm and asks with tear-streaked face, 'Are you still here? Will you stay with me until it's light? Are you disgusted with me because I'm little and afraid? Are you going to give me away?' and you are grieved and saddened over the child's lack of trust, do you realize that you do the same thing to Me? Or don't you believe that I am at least as sensitive a father as you?

"Do you understand the word of My Son: 'I do nothing by myself. I do only what I see my Father doing' (John 8:28)? Who do you think first wept over Jerusalem when they refused to receive My own Son?

"Do you claim to know what We shared when Jesus withdrew to a mountaintop and spent the night with Me alone? Do you know whence came the inspiration to wash the feet of the Twelve? Or is that below My dignity, distant Oriental magistrate that I am? Do you understand that motivated by love alone your God became your slave in the Upper Room? Remember, 'I do only what I see my Father doing.'

"Have you grappled with the core question of your faith, which is not 'Is Jesus God-like?' but 'Is God Jesus-like?' Do you comprehend that all the attitudes, values, qualities, and characteristics of My Son are Mine; that he who sees Jesus sees Me, His Father?

"Were you grieved by the divine command to Abraham that he slay his only begotten son Isaac on Mount Moriah? Were you relieved when the angel intervened, Abraham's hand was stayed, and the sacrifice was not carried out? Have you forgotten that on Good Friday no angel intervened, that sacrifice was carried out, and it was not the heart of Abraham that was broken?

"When your friend loses a child temporarily in death, do you go to the funeral home and grieve with him and try to comfort him? When was the last time you grieved with Me and tried to comfort Me on Good Friday? Do you know that My heart was broken on that dark day? That I am your Father, that I feel as much as you?

"Are you aware that I *had* to raise Jesus from the dead on Easter morning because My love is everlasting? That I could not bear the thought of eternity without the presence of My only begotten? Are you serenely confident that I will raise you, too, My adopted son?

"But of course you are aware of all these things. Was it not you who just told Me that it is all old hat, that you know that I love you?"

What is the quality of my faith commitment? Is there movement and development? Is it alive and growing? Faith is a real, personal relationship with Jesus of Nazareth. Like any human love affair, it can never be static, exhausted, terminal, settled. When Scripture, the Eucharist, and ministry become routine, they are moribund. When the Father's love is taken for granted, we paint Him into a corner and rob Him of the opportunity to love us in new and surprising ways. Then faith begins to shrivel and shrink. When I become so spiritually sophisticated that "Abba" is old hat, then the Father has been had, Jesus has been tamed, the Spirit has been domesticated, and the Pentecostal fire has been extinguished. Evangelical faith is the antithesis of cozy, comfortable piety. Faith means you want growing intimacy with Jesus Christ. Cost what it may, you want to want nothing else. The moment I conclude that I can now cope with the awesome love of God, I am dead. I could more easily contain the Gulf of Mexico in a shot glass than I can comprehend the wild, uncontainable love of God.

If our faith is going to be criticized, let it be for the right reasons. Not because we are too emotional but because we are not emotional enough. Not because our passions are so powerful but because they are so puny. Not because we are too affectionate but because we lack a deep, passionate, undivided love for the person of Jesus Christ.

As I write this, I am making a thirty-day silent directed retreat in the snow-covered hills of Pennsylvania. Thanks to my spiritual director, one word has sounded and resounded in my heart this month. Jesus did not say this on Calvary, though He could have, but He is saying it now: "I'm dying to be with you. I'm really dying to be with you." It was as if He were summoning me a second time. I sensed that what I thought I knew was straw. I had barely glimpsed, I hadn't dreamed of what His love could be. His Word drove me deeper into solitude, seeking not the gift of tongues, healing, prophecy or a good religious experience each time I prayed but simply *understanding*, a knowledgeable grip on "the breadth and length and height and depth of Christ's love and experience this love which surpasses all knowledge" (Ephesians 3:18-19).

Perhaps the most fundamental religious question I can ask myself today is: Do I really believe the Good News of Jesus Christ? Do I hear His word spoken to my heart: "Shalom, be at peace. I understand your fears, your failures, your brokenness. I don't expect you to be perfect. I have been there. All is well. You have My love. You don't have to pay for it and you can't deserve it. I expect more failure from you than you expect from yourself. You only have to open and receive it. You only have to say yes to my love—a love beyond anything you can intellectualize or imagine"?

Father, because I am loved
and I love
I don't have to
explain myself to you.
I don't have to
excuse myself to you.
I don't have to
abase myself before you.
You know all about me,
and you call me friend.
You call me your delight.
You call me your beloved.

Because I am loved
and I love
I need not lie prostrate
on my face before you.
I am free to run
into the circle of your waiting arms,
to enter the fullness of your embrace,
to be held
safely
strongly
securely
against your heart.

Because I am loved
and I love
I don't have to worry
about my response or lack of it.
I don't have to struggle
with my desire to understand.
I don't have to wrestle
with my feeling of unworthiness.
All I have to do is
be still,
stay close
and let you love me
into wholeness.

Father, sometimes
it's the hardest thing
in the world
just to be still,
stay close
and let you love me.
But because I am loved
and I love,
I try.

Here I am, Father.
Still, for once.
Closer than I've ever been.
Waiting.
Accepting.
Wanting.
Love me, Father.

CHAPTER 2

HOPING OR WISHFUL THINKING?

*C*losely related to the quality of my faith is the intensity of my hope. The Word of Jesus carries the implicit theme that the world is out to do us good. When you stop and think about it, that's an extraordinary idea. In most of our lives we have the impression that the world has done us considerable harm and comparatively little good. Yet if the Abba of Jesus loves us, if He pursues us as a tremendous Lover[1] who is dying (in His Son) to be with us, then we are committed to the notion that His world, the work of His hands, is out to do us good. And that means taking the risk of letting others do good to us. It means going into the wedding feast and celebrating with the firm conviction that we are not going to be chumped, cheated, or disastrously surprised.

One evening in the late 1970s, I was vacationing at the Jersey shore with my brother (who has since gone home to the Father, but who was always a delightful surprise to be with). Late Saturday afternoon, I took a walk around an artificial lake in Belmar, New Jersey. On the far side was a banquet hall called The Barclay, which hosted parties, conventions, and wedding receptions. More than a hundred people were filing in the front door. They had just left the nuptial liturgy at St. Rose Church and were anticipating the reception. It had already begun. They could hear the music and

---

[1] Francis Thompson, "The Hound of Heaven."

laughter, drinking and dancing inside. The looks on their faces! They were jubilant, keyed up, bursting with impatience, sure of their reserved seats; they couldn't wait to get in. They looked like they were going to a wedding feast.

More than a hundred years ago the atheist philosopher Friedrich Nietzsche reproached a group of Christians: "Yuck, you make me sick!" When their spokesman asked why, he answered, "Because you redeemed don't look like you're redeemed. You're as fearful, guilt-ridden, anxious, confused, and adrift in an alien environment as I am. I'm allowed. I don't believe. I have nothing to hope for. But you people claim you have a Savior. Why don't you look like you are saved?"

In Matthew 22 Jesus described the kingdom of God as a wedding feast. Do you really trust that you are going to a wedding feast that has already begun? Do you really believe that God loves you unconditionally and as you are? Are you committed to the idea that the nature of the world is to be a celebration? If you are, then in the words of Father John Powell, S. J., "Please notify your face."

I am not mincing words here. I am not beating around the bush or indulging in wishful thinking. I am a son of God, and I am going to the kingdom!

Why don't we go in now? Because we know that inside it is not a perfect banquet for the simple fact that we are living between the Cross and the Resurrection. Christianity does not deny the reality of suffering and evil. In 1976, thirty-four men died from the mysterious Legionnaires' disease in Philadelphia. The following week 144 people were swept away in a flash flood in Colorado; nine days later 180,000 people were killed in an earthquake outside of Beijing, China. In the face of such tragedies, the man of hope affirms that the providence of God rules the world, that Jesus is Lord of history, that death is not ultimate but rather the final breakthrough into the waiting, outstretched arms of the Father.

After Jesus came down from the Mount of Transfiguration,

He told His disciples that He was going up to Jerusalem, that He would be executed, and that He would triumph over death. Jesus was not the least bit confident that He would be spared suffering. What He was confident of was vindication. Our hope, our acceptance of the invitation to the banquet is not based on the idea that we are going to be free of pain and suffering. Rather, it is based on the firm conviction that we will triumph over suffering.

Do you believe that you, too, will live? Because that is the meaning of Christian hope. It is not Pollyanna optimism or wishful thinking. It is not something that yields to discouragement, defeat, and frustration. On the contrary, Christian hope stands firm and serene, confident even in the face of the Holocaust, even in the face of terminal cancer. However serious we believe Good Friday is, we are confident that Easter Sunday lies ahead of us. What if we do die? Jesus died too; and if Jesus died, we believe that now He lives and that we shall live too.

The second call of Jesus in our lives is a summons to a more radical leap in hope, an existential commitment to the Good News of the wedding feast. Let us not get lost in abstract theologizing, fuzzy philosophizing, or pious jargon. The fundamental question remains: Is the Word of Jesus Christ true? If an eschatological age has dawned, if God really was present in Jesus in a unique way, if we are privileged to be in intimate contact with the living God on the basis of affectionate familiarity, then our faces should be bright with laughter in the midst of a game we thoroughly enjoy.

Are you really a man or a woman of hope? Hope not merely in some splendid future yet to come but hope in a wedding banquet that is going on right now.

Lord, thank you
for setting me free.
Free to blow bubbles,
fly kites,
listen to seashells,
cuddle kittens,
build castles in the sand,
wish on stars.

Thank you
for setting me free.
Free to hunt for four-leaf clovers,
explore oak trees with inviting branches,
run laughing in the rain,
walk barefoot,
jump puddles,
wave at trains.

Thank you
for setting me free.
Free to yellow my nose in buttercups,
catch a firefly to see his light,
pick the first wild strawberry,
count the stars,
talk to ladybugs,
chase a thistle.

Thank you
for setting me free.
Free to see you in
sunlight dancing on the water,
dogwood smiling at the sky,
willows curtseying to the river,
azaleas flaming across the land,

rainbowed cobwebs,
drifting leaves.

Thank you
for setting me free.
Free to play with,
wonder at
and love
all that you have given me.
And free, as well,
to give it back
to you.

CHAPTER 3

LOVE

An indecisive faith and a wavering hope immobilize us on the journey to fullness of life and the Spirit of Jesus Christ. If we have surrendered to the fact that Jesus was telling the truth, then the world in which we live is really an exciting place. It's a place of romance and adventure, a place of promise and possibility, a place of confidence and joyous expectation. But more than that, our world is a place of love. And the worst sin we can commit is the sin against love.

If we believe in the exciting message of Jesus, if we hope in vindication, there must be love and we must run the risk of being loved. The idea that God is love is certainly not new with Jesus. In fact, it probably wasn't even exclusive to the Judeo-Christian tradition. Other men at other times in other parts of the world have thought or hoped or wished that the living God might actually love them. But Jesus added a note of confidence. He didn't say that maybe God is love—or that it would be nice if God were love. He said: *God is love—period*. But there is more to the message of Jesus. He insisted that His Father is crazy with love, that God is a kooky God who can scarcely bear to be without us. The parable that makes this truth so obvious is that of the prodigal son, or as they say in Scripture these days, the parable of the loving father (see Luke 15:11-32).

The emphasis is not on the sinfulness of the son but on the generosity of the father. We ought to reread this parable periodically if only to catch the delicate nuance at the first meeting between the two. The son had his little speech of sorrow carefully rehearsed. It was an elegant, polished statement of sorrow. But the old man didn't let him finish it. The son had barely arrived on the scene when suddenly a fine new robe was thrown over his shoulders. He heard music, the fatted calf was being carried into the parlor, and he didn't even have a chance to say to his father, "I'm sorry."

The theme is that God wants us back even more than we could possibly want to be back and that we don't have to go into great detail about our sorrow. All you have to do, the parable says, is appear on the scene; before you get a chance to run away again, the Father grabs you by your new robe and pulls you into the banquet so you can't get away.

There is a fascinating passage in chapter 8 of John's gospel about the woman caught in sin. Remember how the crowd dragged her before Jesus and asked, "What do we do about her? She was caught in adultery. Moses says we should stone her, but the Romans won't let us stone people. What do you think?"

Jesus just ignored them and began to write in the sand. Then He looked up and said, "Well, let the one here who hasn't committed any sin throw the first rock." One by one they drifted away. Then Jesus said to the woman, "Is there no one here to condemn you?" She replied, "No one, Lord." He answered, "Okay, go, and don't commit this sin anymore."

Now get the picture. Jesus didn't ask her if she was sorry. He didn't demand a firm purpose of amendment. He didn't seem too concerned that she might dash back into the arms of her lover. She just stood there, and Jesus gave her absolution before she asked for it.

That particular passage was so scandalous in the early church that though it is certainly part of an ancient gospel tradition, it didn't get included in the gospel story for almost a hundred years. All the Scripture scholars say that passage does not belong in John's gospel. The language is completely different. It's a much older tradition and so on. But it didn't get incorporated in John's gospel until after his death because it was scandalous. The early Christian moralists had a much stricter idea of good and evil than Jesus did, so they tried to hush up this incident because it made Jesus look too lenient.

And that's the nature of God's love for us—a love that is positively scandalous, a love that's embarrassing. Why doesn't this God of ours display some taste and discretion in dealing with us? Why doesn't He show more restraint? To be perfectly blunt about it, couldn't God arrange to have a little more dignity? Wow!

Now, if we were in His position, we'd know perfectly well how to behave, and the prodigal son would have recited his speech down to the very last word. And when he finished, we would have said, "Well, you go away, prodigal son, and I'll think about this for two or three weeks. Then you'll be informed by parcel post whether or not I've decided to let you back on the farm."

I don't think anyone here would have approved of throwing rocks at the poor woman in adultery, but we would have made darn sure that she presented a detailed act of contrition and was very firm in her purpose of amendment. Because if we let her off without her saying she was sorry, wouldn't she be back into adultery before sunset?

No, the love of our God isn't dignified at all, and apparently that's the way He expects our love to be. Not only does He require us to accept His kooky, embarrassing kind of love, but once we've accepted it, He expects us to behave the same way with others. I suppose I could live, if I had to, with a God whose love for us is embarrassing. But the thought that I've got to act that way with other people—that's a bit too much to swallow.

Perhaps the simplest, though certainly not the easiest, place to start is with myself. Carl Jung, the great psychiatrist, once reflected that we are all familiar with these words of Jesus: "Whatever you do to the least of my brethren, that you do unto me" (Matthew 25:40). Then Jung asked a very probing question: "What if you discovered that the least of the brethren of Jesus, the one who needs your love the most, the one you can help the most by loving, the one to whom your love will be most meaningful — what if you discovered that this least of the brethren of Jesus . . . is *you?*"

Then do for yourself what you would do for others. And that wholesome self-love that Jesus enjoined when He said, "Love your neighbor as yourself," might begin with the simple acknowledgment, "What is the story of my priesthood? It is the story of an unfaithful man through whom God continues to work!" That word is not only consoling; it is freeing, especially for those of us caught up in the oppression of thinking that God can work only through saints. What a word of healing, forgiveness, and comfort it is for many of us priests who have discovered that we are earthen vessels who fulfill Jesus' prophecy: "I tell you solemnly, this day, this night, before the cock crows twice, you will have disowned me three times."

The Lord is now calling me a second time, affirming me, enabling me, encouraging me, challenging me all the way into fullness of faith, hope, and love in the power of His Holy Spirit. Ignorant, weak, sinful man that I am, with easy rationalizations for my sinful behavior, I am being told anew in the unmistakable language of love, "I am with you, I am for you, I am in you. I expect more failure from you than you expect from yourself."

There is one sin against love that deserves special mention because it is so crucial to the second call of Jesus Christ: procrastination. That is, putting things off, wasting the energies of life and love that are within us. You don't have to be in the ministry long to discover that most of us spend considerable time putting off the things we should be doing or would like to do or want to do — but are afraid to do. We are afraid of failure. We don't like it; we shun it, avoid it because of our inordinate desire to be thought well of by others. So we come up with a thousand brilliant excuses for doing nothing. And the judgment of the Lord High Executioner in *The Mikado* on the girl who perpetually procrastinated falls on us — "She'll never be missed; no, she'll never be missed!"

Each of us pays a heavy price for our fear of falling flat on our faces. It assures the progressive narrowing of our personalities and prevents exploration and experimentation. As we get older, we do only the things we do well. There is no growth in Christ Jesus without some difficulty and fumbling. If we are going to keep on growing, we must keep on risking failure throughout our lives. When Max Planck was awarded the Nobel prize for the discovery of the quantum theory, he said, "Looking back over the long and labyrinthine path which finally led to the discovery, I am vividly reminded of Goethe's saying that men will always be making mistakes as long as they are striving after something."

You know, in spite of the fact that Christianity speaks of the cross, redemption, and sin, we're unwilling to admit failure in our lives. Why? Partially, I guess, because it's human nature's defense mechanism against its own inadequacies. But even more so, it's because of the successful image our culture demands of us. There are some real problems with projecting the perfect image. First of all, it's simply not true—we are not always happy, optimistic, in command. Second, projecting the flawless image keeps us from reaching people who feel we just wouldn't understand them. And third, even if we could live a life with no conflict, suffering, or mistakes, it would be a shallow existence. The Christian with depth is the person who has failed and learned to live with his failure.

Procrastination is perhaps the worst, the most damaging failure of all. We who believe in Jesus, who hope in vindication, who proclaim the love of the heavenly Father waste our time trying to avoid the things that are most important because we're afraid we are going to fail in them. How much faith, how much hope, how much love does the perpetual procrastinator really have?

As you go through life, if you acquire any self-awareness, any kind of honest insight into your own personality, you know pretty well what your weaknesses are. You know how you are going to evade the responsibility of faith, hope, and love that Jesus offers. If you're honest, you know that you can't scapegoat—that you can't say it was somebody else's fault. We know that when it comes time for rendering an account of our lives, we will be blamed or praised not for what the television evangelist has done, not for what the bishop has done, not for what the pastor has done (unless we are the pastor) — we will be blamed or praised according to whether or not we have accepted the invitation to believe the message.

In the final analysis, the real challenge of Christian growth is personal responsibility. The Spirit of Jesus calls out a second time. Are you going to take charge of your life today? Are you going to be responsible for what you do? Are you going to believe not because you are forced to believe in the Good News but because you want to believe it? Are you going to hope not because people say you should hope but because you are confident of vindication? Are you going to love not because it is a commandment but because it is a joy? Are you going into that banquet because you really believe there are festivities inside? Are you going into that banquet Jesus invited you to in His Father's name? Or in an act of heroic but misguided responsibility, are you going to say, "I'm sorry, Jesus, but I don't think I'm going to like Your party"?

Perhaps we are all in the position of the man in Morton Kelsey's story who came to the edge of an abyss that he couldn't cross. As he stood there wondering what to do next, he was amazed to discover a tightrope stretched across the abyss. And slowly, surely, across the rope came an acrobat pushing before him a wheelbarrow with another performer in it. When they finally reached the safety of solid ground, the acrobat smiled at the man's amazement. "Don't you think I can do it again?" The acrobat put his question again; when the answer was the same, he pointed to the wheelbarrow and said, "Good! Then get in and I will take you across."[1]

What did the traveler do? This is just the question we have to ask ourselves about Jesus Christ. Do we state our belief in Him

---

[1] Morton Kelsey, *The Other Side of Silence* (Mahwah, NJ: Paulist, 1976), 54.

in no uncertain terms, even in finely articulated creeds, and then refuse to get into the wheelbarrow? What we do about the Lordship of Jesus is a better indication of our faith than what we think.

What the world longs for from the Christian faith is the witness of men and women daring enough to be different, humble enough to make mistakes, wild enough to be burnt in the fire of love, real enough to make others see how unreal they are.

Jesus, Son of the living God, anoint us with fire this day. Let Your Word not shine in our hearts but let it burn. Let there be no division, compromise, or holding back. Separate the mystics from the romantics and goad us to that daredevil leap into the abyss of Your love. Let the prayer of Nikos Kazantzakis arise from our hearts as a passionate pitch of loving awareness:

I am a bow in your hands, Lord.
Draw me, lest I rot.
Do not overdraw me, Lord. I shall break.
Overdraw me, Lord, and who cares if I break?

Lord, you're the most unpredictable
person
I know.
Just when I think
I've finally begun
to figure you out,
you do something
so fantastic,
so completely, wildly
unexpected
that I'm knocked for a loop.

I think I know where to find you
and then suddenly I find you
in the most unlikely places;
at the oddest moments;
in the strangest people.

I think I know your voice;
and then I hear you
in a child's crooning lullaby;
in an old man's chuckle;
in a lover's sigh.

I think I know your face;
and then I see you
in a psychiatric ward;
in a jam-packed tenement;
in the streets,
wandering aimlessly.

I think I know you well;
and then I discover
I know you not at all.

I think I know your love;
and then I discover
I haven't begun to know it.

Thank you, Lord,
for being unpredictable.
Thank you for startling me
out of my comfortable rut.
Continue teaching me
that you're a God
of infinite surprises.

CHAPTER 4

THE BEAUTY OF THE EUCHARISTIC LITURGY

I have seen some beautiful things recently. Hitchhiking across the Italian Alps, I saw a snow-covered peak at dawn. In Florence, I stood for two hours before Michelangelo's *David* with my mouth open, unconscious of time; I was abruptly told by a guard that the museum was closing and it was time to leave. Running along the Jersey shore, I saw a fiery sun falling into the gathering darkness. We first experience beauty usually in the things that surround us. Sometimes in sensible things, other times in the transparency of a look or a glance that reveals a soul full of light. Whenever we encounter the beautiful, our hearts awaken, stir, quicken, thrill because there is an extraordinary magic power in the least thing: a tiny plant burgeoning in spring, a shade of the sky at a given moment of the day, a calm, cold night brilliant with star shine—all things that ravish the heart. They're a small taste of Paradise Lost on an earth where so many things are torn and tearing. They are little oases in the vast wasteland of the world.

St. Augustine in his commentary on Psalm 148, "God is made manifest by the heavens and the earth," asked, "Does God proclaim Himself in these wonders?" And he replied,

No, all things proclaim Him, all things speak. Their beauty is the voice by which they announce God, by which they sing, "It is you who made me beautiful, not me myself but you." When do the heavens and the earth cry aloud like that? At the moment you discover what they conceal. It's your reflection upon them, it's the attention with which you regard them, that opens their voices to cry aloud, "How beautiful is the One who made us." Remember Jesus who never ceased to marvel at the beauty of creatures: "See that lily over there. I tell you Solomon in all his glory never looked as beautiful as that."

Cardinal Newman related that as a child he imagined that behind every flower there was an angel who made it grow and blossom. Later in life he wrote, "The reality is more profound. It is God Himself who can be discovered in the beauty of sensible things."

Even more striking, more arresting is the new world of beauty revealed in the dignity of a human soul by a word, a glance, a gesture. I'm thinking of the beggar in Moliere's *Don Juan*. He sits at the corner of the street as a nobleman passes. It's Don Juan, a bitter man, both his fortune and his character ruined. "An alms for the love of God," cries the beggar. Don Juan stops, reaches in his pocket, and holds out his last gold coin over the outstretched arms of the beggar. "Blaspheme God and I'll give it to you." The beggar drops his hands. "No, my Lord," he says quietly. "I shall not blaspheme." That's all. But so splendid. A gesture like that is more beautiful than a heaven full of stars, a thousand symphonies, a *David*, an Eiffel Tower, or a *Mona Lisa*. St. Thomas said that the splendor of a just soul is so seductive that it surpasses the beauty of all created things.

It is hard to speak of beauty without speaking of St. Francis. In his personality was mirrored a generous measure of the transcendent beauty of God. If God is an illimitable ocean of beauty, Francis was a small spring shooting up, such as the world had never seen before. His gestures were the revelation of his soul. One day he arrived in the village square. A large crowd followed him. As everyone knew, the village priest had not been living a life of rectitude. As Francis reached the square, the priest by chance happened out of the church. The crowd watched and waited. What would Francis do? Denounce the priest for the scandal he had created, sermonize the villagers on human frailty and the need for compassion, simply pretend he didn't see the priest and continue on his way? No. He stepped forward, knelt in the mud, took the priest's hand, and kissed it. That's all. And that is magnificent. Toward the end of his life, Francis gathered two branches—one represented a violin, the other a bow. And what a marvelous melody he played. Interiorly, of course. But what is the music of Mozart and Bach beside this? The words and gestures of Francis were manifestations of a soul completely surrendered to God. As we see the beauty streaming from his soul, one realizes anew the truth of the words of French novelist Leon Bloy: "The only real sadness in life is not to be a saint."

It is commonplace to say this woman is attractive or that one is stunning because of a slender figure and fine features, but a beautiful woman transmits a loveliness that clothes and cosmetics, shape and facial features could never create. The eighteenth-century French saint Benedict Joseph Labre by common standards was an ugly man. Yet it is said that everywhere he went, street painters begged him to pose for a portrait, completely enamored by the transparent beauty of his emaciated, recollected face. Great holiness seduces artists too—at least those who have learned to recognize and admire human dignity.

The Greek and Latin fathers of the church posed the question—could the beauty of Jesus have endured while He suffered all that was foretold of the Suffering Servant in the prophecy of Isaiah: A Man of Sorrows, murdered for us; bloodied, despised, disfigured, a worm and not a man, who knew the nadir of the agony such as no man has ever dreamed? Was the Crucifixion really beautiful? For those who saw only the external tragedy, Jesus naked and nailed, flanked by two criminals, blood streaming from every wound and pore of His body, it was a horrible spectacle indeed. And for that reason, with the advent of Constantine, crucifixion was abolished as brutalizing and inhuman. But there is more to the death of Jesus than just that. There is the luminous, transcendent, interior beauty of His soul, and we must never forget it. The body of Jesus was racked, broken, bathed in blood, but His soul was ennobled by a dignity, suffused with a love that illuminated, transformed, and transfigured His suffering and death. This was the mightiest act of love ever to rise from a human soul. Surely the Crucifixion was a brutal, dehumanizing atrocity exteriorly, but it was beautiful because of the sentiments in Jesus' soul — unwavering obedience to the glory of His Father and illimitable love for men. It was because of these dispositions at the moment of His last breath that this last breath won reparation for our sins and achieved our redemption. "Never forget," said St. Cyril of Alexandria, "that what gives value to a sacrifice is not the renouncement it demands but the degree of love which inspires the renouncement." What of the beauty of Jesus on the cross then? The angels could contemplate it. Jesus was disfigured, but something transfigured all. At that moment, the human soul of Jesus ravished the heart of His heavenly Father because of the wild generosity of its love. Can you contemplate the Cross, see Jesus in the throes of His death agony, beaten and bullied, scourged and spat upon by a crowd of brutes, hear Him say, "Father, forgive them for they know not what they do," and not be awed by the loveliness of this Person?

What of our Eucharistic celebrations? Are they beautiful in the eyes of the Father? Answer no if the songs, words, and gestures are rubrical niceties and liturgical novelties sapped of any interiority. Then, in the words of Paul, even though you are filled with all knowledge and a faith that could move mountains, your Eucharist is sounding brass and tinkling cymbal. But answer yes if word, music, and movement are the outward expression of the inner attitude of your souls, if they are the overflow of the wild generosity of your love, if your hearts are fused with Christ's as He renews in an unbloody way the drama of Calvary. *The beauty of the Eucharistic liturgy, like that of Calvary, is essentially interior.*

Lord, I'm not free—
but who wants to be?
You're all that
matters
in my life.
I don't want to be free
of my hunger
for your bread.
I don't want to be free
of my thirst
for your word.
I don't want to be free
of my desire
for your will.
I don't want to be free
of my longing
for your presence.
I don't want to be free
of my need
to be taken up,
taken over,
joined to you.

Lord, may I never
be free
from wanting you.

CHAPTER 5

CHRISTMAS REFLECTIONS AT O'HARE

*I*t's an icy winter's night, and O'Hare International Airport is in bedlam. All flights are canceled. Visibility is poor due to fog, frost, and freezing rain. Thousands of people are clustered at the ticket counters; some clamoring for redress, others wrapped in stoic silence. Children are crying, the PA system is blaring, and the defeated are bellying up to the bar. I'm in mild turmoil. How can the Good News be proclaimed in Dallas if the weather won't shape up in Chicago?

Across the aisle sits a middle-aged black woman cradling a child. It's more than a serene smile playing at the corners of her mouth. She's laughing. She's actually laughing? Intrigued I cross the aisle and find myself staring at the woman. She is rubbing her fingers across the child's lips as he blows mightily "brrh, brrh." She looks up.

"Ma'am, you're the only person in this place who seems to be together. Would you mind telling me why you're so happy?"

"Sho," she said. "Christmas is coming and dat Jesus—He make me laugh!"

I thanked her, recrossed the aisle, and slumped into my seat. "Dat Jesus—He make me laugh!" I repeated. Am I getting too serious about life? In the hurly-burly of the marketplace have I let my childlike sense of wonder fade? Have I stopped looking at sunsets and rainbows? Am I so lost in preaching, teaching, writing, traveling that I no longer hear the sound of rain on the roof? How long since I stopped making snowballs and flying kites? Am I interpreting the charismatic prophecies of trial and tribulation, desolation and deprivation as a death sentence? Am I growing uncomfortable with Jesus telling me to model my life after the birds and the flowers? Am I irritated with people, like the woman across the aisle, who don't seem to realize how serious life really is? Has getting serious about life meant becoming sad about life? Is *living* just another word for *endurance*?

In seminary I was taught that *Isaac* (*Yishaq* in Hebrew) means "laughter." Abraham and his wife, Sarah, gave up on God's promise of a child. When Sarah was told that she would soon be pregnant, she laughed in disbelief. But God had the last laugh. A son was born to them in their old age, and the human laughter of despair turned into the Father's laughter of love. They named their son Isaac—laughter—for he was a sign of the triumph of God's levity over man's gravity.

Isaac, son of the promise made to Abraham, is a prophetic foreshadowing of Jesus, in whom the promise is fulfilled. Jesus is God's final laughter. Laughter is the celebration of incongruity. Nothing could be more incongruous in the Hebrew tradition than the enfleshment of the Word by a virgin.

Christmas is the promise that the God who came in history and comes daily in mystery will one day come in glory. God is saying in Jesus that in the end everything will be all right. Nothing can harm you permanently, no suffering is irrevocable, no loss is lasting, no defeat is more than transitory, no disappointment is conclusive. Jesus did not deny the reality of suffering, discouragement, disappointment, frustration, and death; He simply stated that the kingdom of God would conquer all of these horrors, that the Father's love is so prodigal that no evil could possibly resist it.

Christmas is a vision that enables the Christian to see beyond the tragic in his life. It is a reminder that he needs the laughter of God to prevent him from taking the world too seriously. The Christian law of levity says that whatever falls into the earth will rise again. God's laughter is His loving act of salvation, and Christian laughter is the echo of Christmas joy in us.

If you really accept the mystery of Bethlehem, "glad tidings of great joy," your heart will be filled with the laughter of the Father. "You are sad now, but I shall see you again, and your hearts will be full of joy, and that joy no one shall take from you" (John 16:22).

O, Carey Landry, is this what you had in mind when you wrote that lyrical melody on the *Abba, Father* album, "And the Father will dance as on a day of joy"?

As Advent draws to a close, go to the Father and ask Him, "Abba, why are You dancing?" See Him extend His right hand to the manger in the city of David and say, "Christmas is coming and dat Jesus—He make Me laugh!"

I pray you have a beautiful Christmas, Ho-Ho!

Lord, for a long time
I thought of you
as a man
who never smiled.
I'm afraid
a lot of people
still think of you
that way,
and that's unfortunate.

Because a man
who never smiled at all
would have to be

less than human.
And that's what the
Good News
is all about—
that you became a man.

Lord, I know
you must have smiled a lot.

I know you must have smiled
at children at their play;
as they clambered up
into your lap;
as they hung on your robe
and clung to your hands.

I know you must have smiled
at the sight of lambs
frolicking in the hills
as you made your way
from village to village.

I know you must have smiled
encouragingly
at all those people
who came to you,
frightened and worried,
but seeking,
trusting,
believing.

I know you must have smiled
with pleasure

at the beauty of the world
you had created.

I know you must have smiled
reassuringly and confidently
at your disciples
as they sat and listened
to your words.

I know you must have smiled
often and lovingly
at your mother.

Lord, I know you smile on us.
And your smile
is brighter than the sun.
When the days seem dark and dismal,
and everything looks black,
help us, Lord,
to remember
the glory of your smile.

FORGIVENESS

"Forgive us our trespasses as we forgive those who trespass against us."

This petition in the Lord's Prayer is preceded by the prayer "Thy will be done." The will of our heavenly Father is that we forgive even as we are forgiven, that we be generous with others as God is with us.

There is considerable discussion in the church today about what it means to be charismatic or Spirit-filled. Sometimes the remark "He is in the Spirit" implies that he prays in tongues or gives powerful prophecies or inspirational homilies or possesses the gift of healing. The only sign I know given by Jesus that a person is filled with the Holy Spirit is found in Matthew 5:

> You have heard the commandment, "You shall love your countryman but hate your enemy." My command to you is this: love your enemies, pray for your persecutors. *This will prove that you are children of your heavenly Father, for his sun rises on the bad and the good, he rains on the just and the unjust.* (verses 43-45, emphasis added)

No one can be a son or daughter of the Abba of Jesus without being anointed by the Holy Spirit. "*The proof* that you are children is that God has sent forth into our hearts the Spirit of His Son which cries out, '*Abba*, Father!' You are no longer a slave but a child! And the fact that you are a child makes you an heir of the kingdom by God's design" (Galatians 4:6-7, emphasis added).

In "The Pater Noster as an Eschatological Prayer," the eminent Bible scholar Raymond E. Brown said, "The reason that the Christian can even pose this petition [Forgive us our trespasses . . .] is his consciousness of the Fatherhood of God."[1]

The proof par excellence of the Christian who has experienced God's unbearable forgiveness and infinite patience is that he is able to be forgiving and patient with others. Whatever other gifts he may possess, this sign given by Jesus stamps his life as being "in the Spirit."

The author Francis MacNutt said, "If the Lord Jesus Christ has washed you in His own blood and forgiven you all your sins, how dare you refuse to forgive yourself?" Self-hatred is a sin. Anything that causes division in the body of Christ is sinful. When I am divided within myself, when I am so preoccupied with my own sins, egocentricity, and moral failures that I cannot hear the anguished cry of others, then I have subtly reestablished self as the center of my focus and concern. Biblically, that is idolatry.

Recently a man approached me in the terminal of the Kansas City International Airport and asked, "Father, may I go to confession?" He began by revealing that he was a priest. Then, broken with grief, he spoke of his twelve-year estrangement from God, his life of drinking, debauchery, hypocrisy, self-hatred. The tears rolled down his cheeks. His confession was heavy, heavy, heavy. Midway through, I reached out and embraced him, crying, "Stop, for God's sake, stop. No more. He sees your heart and understands. All your sins are forgiven. Be at peace and don't sin anymore." With both of us in tears, I asked him to pray Psalm 116 in thanksgiving, gave him absolution, and departed. Sitting on the plane en route to Des Moines, I asked myself, "Brennan, would you do for yourself what you just did for your brother?" Then I heard the

---

[1]   Raymond E. Brown, "The Pater Noster as an Eschatological Prayer," *New Testament Essays* (Milwaukee, WI: Bruce Pub. Co., 1965).

words of priest/psychologist Adrian van Kaam as if for the first time: "Gentleness towards my precious, fragile self as called forth uniquely by God constitutes the core of my gentleness with others and is the main condition for my presence to God."

Through the help of Father Francis Martin during a Scripture course at Loyola in New Orleans, I learned that the only four places in the New Testament where the phrase "Thy will be done" occurs are in the context of *martyrdom*. In Matthew 26:42, Mark 14:36, and Luke 22:42, Jesus is in the Garden of Gethsemane. As He approaches His martyrdom, He prays to His beloved Abba, "Let Your will be done, not mine." And He fulfills His Father's will on Calvary, praying, "Father, forgive them, for they do not know what they are doing" (Luke 23:34, NIV).

Again in Acts 21:13-14, Paul announced that he was ready for martyrdom: "Why are you crying and breaking my heart in this way? For in the name of the Lord Jesus, I am prepared, not only for imprisonment, but for death, in Jerusalem." Since he would not be dissuaded, he said nothing further except "The Lord's will be done."

Colleen McCullough's best-selling novel *The Thorn Birds* begins with the legend of a bird that sings only once in its life — and it sings more sweetly than any other creature on the face of the earth. From the moment the bird leaves her nest, she searches for a thorn tree, refusing to rest until she has found one. Then singing among the savage branches, she impales herself upon the longest and sharpest thorn. And dying, she rises above her own agony to outcarol, outsing the lark and the nightingale.

A superlative song — existence the price.

The whole world stills to listen and the Abba of Jesus smiles, for the best is bought at the price of great pain.

At this moment in my own personal legend, martyrdom does not seem to require marching to the lions for Christ or bringing Him to Zaire or Nicaragua as a missionary. The call I hear deep within me is to reveal His forgiving love to those who have trespassed against me. It costs a lot to pray, "Thy will be done" — death to the old man, overcoming grudges and long-standing resentments, transcending bitter memories and justifiable hostilities, reaching out in reconciliation to those who have turned me down, ripped me off, and screwed me up.

Maybe this is why the only four times that "Thy will be done" occurs in the New Testament is in the context of martyrdom. The older I get, the more I realize the truth of the adage "It's easier to die for Christ than to live for Him."

Lord, deliver me from
self-righteous people.
Deliver me from people
who think they know you
better than anyone else.
Who think that only they
can understand your ways.
Who think that only they
can interpret your word.
Who wail and gnash their teeth
over the sins of the world,
but fail to see their own.

Who urge others to meekness
and humility,
but fail to follow
their own advice.

Who expound at length
on charity
but fail to practice it.
Who preach mercy and
compassion,
but fail to show it.
Who insist that they alone
hold the key
that unlocks the door
to your kingdom.
Who insist that they alone
have found the sure path
by which to follow you.

Lord, deliver me from myself.
I, too, am one of these.

CHAPTER 7

PLEASE TEST THIS PROPHECY

*S*o sparingly have I been used by the Lord in the prophetic ministry (three times in ten years, I think), I do not possess what St. Paul called "a tested gift" (see 1 Thessalonians 5:19-21). Perhaps these words were intended only for myself. So I submit the following story to the reader's discernment. If it arouses your mind and stirs your heart, then do whatever obedience to the Word requires.

The story begins with this reflection: "The prime cause for the westward migration of the Delaware and Shawnee Indians from the Susquehanna to the Ohio was the debauchery caused by the rum traffic of white Indian traders."[1]

Again and again wise chiefs of the tribe filed complaint against the traffic that was robbing their hunters of their furs, their warriors of their manhood, and their women of their virtue. But the rum continued to flow and penetrated most Indian villages. Chiefs continually objected to the sale of the rum, which they considered the white man's most awful curse. Their objections were in vain. Traders steadily grew wealthy, and Indians began to live dissipated lives.

In an attempt to stop the white Indian traders from debauching his people, Scarouady, an Oneida chieftain and friend of the

---

[1] George P. Donehoo, "Carlisle and the Red Man of Other Days."

English colonists, made a speech at the first Indian council at Carlisle, Pennsylvania, on September 28, 1753.

> We desire that Pennsylvania and Virginia should forbear settling our lands over the Allegheny Hills. We advise rather to call your people back to this side of the Hills, lest damage be done and you think ill of us. . . .
>
> Your traders now bring little powder and lead and other valuable goods. The rum ruins us. We beg you would prevent its coming in such great quantities by regulating the traders. When these whisky traders come, they bring thirty or forty kegs and put them down before us and make us drunk, and get all the skins that should go to pay the debts we have contracted for goods bought of the fair traders, and by this means we not only ruin ourselves but the fair traders as well. These wicked whisky sellers, once they have got the Indians in liquor, make them sell the very clothes from their backs. In short, if this practice be continued, we must inevitably be ruined.[2]

What do I bring to my parish community, my prayer community? Powder and other valuable goods such as compassion, patience, love, deep faith, a prayerful spirit?

Or the whisky that will ruin it? The rum of a quarrelsome spirit, a disillusioned disposition, a tongue dipped in acid, bitter memories, indifference, a cynical smile, a skeptical attitude, an unloving heart?

We all come to the Christian community as traders seeking deeper faith, inner peace, a strong sense of God's presence, the support, encouragement, and understanding of our brothers and sisters. In exchange, we offer an open mind, a grateful heart, a

---

[2] Taken from *Touch the Earth: A Self-Portrait of Indian Existence,* compiled by T. C. McLuhan.

gentle spirit, compassion for the broken, encouragement for the weak, support for the strong, friendship for all, and a hunger for God.

We come not to burden the brethren, not to drive them from the Susquehanna to the Ohio, not from our praying community to another, not to damage them so they will think ill of us, but to build the body by bearing their burdens, lightening their spirits, enriching their faith, making it easier for them to believe, to trust, and to love. Manipulation, power ploys, cliques, preoccupation with ourselves are forgotten, abandoned, and transformed into a wholehearted concern for the glory of God and the good of the brethren.

No, I cannot migrate from the Susquehanna to the Ohio because, as the Little Prince replied to the fox, "*Je suis responsable de ma rose.*" I am responsible for those I love. If I and others depart and the practice continues, the community will inevitably be ruined. There are wicked whisky sellers, false friends who laugh when we laugh but not weep when we hurt. There are selfish traders who profit from our wisdom, our spiritual gifts, our strength but who disappear when we are confused, divided, or rejected.

It is not my own word I speak but the Word of the One who sent me. It is the Lord Jesus Christ calling His people to unity—that they all may be one—as You, Father, are in me, and I in Thee, that they may be perfected in unity, that the world may believe that You have sent me.

"I call you, My people, to rekindle the fire of your love, the love that keeps no score of wrongs, that does not debate who was the offender and who the offended; to the martyrdom of forgiving love: dying to pride, stubbornness, and self-righteousness; to rise to harmony, unity, and brotherhood. I adjure you anew: love one another as I have loved you—a love that led to allowing them to nail Me to the wood, that you might be reconciled to God and to one another. While you were still My enemies, I loved you; I became a naked man with nothing, stripped of everything in a poverty you will never know.

"You must not permit cool cordiality and polite indifference to masquerade as My love for My people. This is not a joke in My eyes; it is no light matter to Me that I have loved you.

"Open your hearts to My Spirit. As you hear this prophetic word, I am filling you with the same love with which I have loved you, so that you may love one another in Me and with Me and through Me to the praise of My Father.

"I am setting you free, My brother, My sister, this moment. I am leading you out of the bondage of self-pity and self-hatred into the freedom of God's children. I am dissipating darkness and discouragement, I am banishing gloom and pessimism from your heart, I am healing division and dissension. I am liberating you, My people, from pettiness, envy, jealousy, and insensitivity. I am drawing you together in My love. I am leading you Myself into the Promised Land of peace and concord where My little ones dwell in harmony, forgiving, accepting, and loving one another.

"In poverty of spirit and purity of heart you shall serve Me and honor Me and raise My name above this city that the world may know that you belong to Me, that I am in the Father and the Father in Me, and that the nations will know that He has sent Me. It is the Lord who speaks to *you,* people of My Blood, purchased at great price. You are Mine, you belong to Me, and no one shall tear you from My hand — *no one.* Neither the world nor the flesh nor the Devil nor the masters of worldly argument nor the false prophets; not the power of hell itself will tear you from My hand or divide you among yourselves."

> Be at peace among yourselves. . . . You must all think of what is best for each other and for the community. Be happy at all times; pray constantly; and for all things give thanks to God, because this is what God expects of you in Christ Jesus. (1 Thessalonians 5:14-18)

Praise you, Father, for your People.
For old people, young people;
tall people, short people;
wise people, simple people;
black people, white people,
red, yellow and brown people
(and green and blue ones, too,
if there are any,
and all shades in between
that we don't know about).

Praise you, Father, for making us,
your children,
in so many varieties.
Praise you for making each of us
so different,
for making each one of us
unique.

Father, don't let us use those
differences
as a cause for
barriers
between us.
Teach us to rejoice
and delight in them
as you do.

CHAPTER 8

ONLY A SHADOW

Recommendation to the Reader: Wherever you see the word *Israel*, replace it with your own name.

Israel, how could I give you up?
My heart turns against it. . . .
When Israel was a child I loved him,
I myself taught him to walk.
I took him in my arms;
Yet he has not understood that I was looking after him.
I led him with reins of kindness,
with leading strings of love.
I was like someone who lifts an infant close up against
his cheek;
stooping down to him I gave him his food. . . .
How could I treat you like Admah,
or deal with you like Zeboim?
My heart recoils from it,
my whole being trembles at the thought.
I will not give reign to my fierce anger,
I will not destroy Ephraim again,
for I am God, not man:
I am the holy one in your midst
and have no wish to destroy. (Hosea 11:1,3-4,8-9)

In the wilderness, too, you saw him:
how the LORD carried you, as a man carries his child,
all along the road you travelled on the road to this place.
(Deuteronomy 1:31)

This is why I am going to lure her
and lead her out into the wilderness
and speak to her heart.
I am going to give her back her vineyards
and make the valley of Achor a gateway of hope.
There she will respond to me as she did when she was young,
as she did when she came out of the land of Egypt.
(Hosea 2:14-17)

The LORD called me from the womb, from the body of
my mother.
He named my name. (Isaiah 49:1)

Does a woman forget her baby at the breast, or fail to
cherish the son of her womb? Yet even if these forget,
I will never forget you. See I have branded you on the
palms of my hands, your ramparts are always under my
eye. (Isaiah 49:14-15)

In the face of all this, what is there left to say? If God
is for us, who can be against us? He who did not hesi-
tate to give us what was most precious to Himself—gave
him as a matter of fact over into our hands—can we not
trust such a God to give us, with him, everything else
we need? . . . I have become absolutely convinced that
neither death nor life, neither messenger of heaven nor
monarch of earth, neither what happens today nor what
may happen tomorrow, neither a power from on high nor

a power from below, nor anything else in God's whole world has any power to separate us from the love of God in Christ Jesus our Lord. (Romans 8:31-34,38-39)

In light of these passages, reflect on the words of Father Carey Landry's beautiful song "Only a Shadow":

My own belief in you, my Lord, is only a shadow of your faith in me, only a shadow of all that will be when we meet face-to-face. . . . The love I have for you, my Lord, is only a shadow of your love for me, only a shadow of all that will be when we meet face-to-face.

Lord, thank you
for not giving up on me.
Thank you
for not washing your hands of me.
Thank you
for not turning your back on me and my brokenness.

Lord, thank you
for not considering me
a hopeless case;
for not shrugging your shoulders
and walking away
from my innumerable failures,
great and small.

Lord, thank you
for believing in me
when I can't believe in myself.

Thank you
for hoping in me
when I can't hope in myself.
Thank you
for trusting me
when I can't trust myself.

Thank you, Lord,
for being my Father
who believes in me,
who hopes in me,
who trusts me
and loves me
forever and ever—
no matter what.

Lord, forgive me for thinking
that your love for me
and my love for you
can be measured
with the same
yardstick.

Your love for me
doesn't depend
on what I do for you,
Your love for me
doesn't falter
in the face
of silence.
Your love for me
doesn't shrivel
in the face
of my refusal to respond.

Your love for me
doesn't use me,
force me,
manipulate me
or coerce me.
Your love for me
is free,
and it sets me free.

Forgive me, Lord,
for trying to do to you
what your love
won't allow you
to do to me.

And even now
you say to me,
"Throw away
that yardstick!"

Lord, I'm so happy
that you're God!

CHAPTER 9

A MIND-BLOWING
PARABLE

A Jewish friend of mine, who converted to Catholic Christianity several years ago, wrote to Raphael Simon — Trappist monk, internationally known psychiatrist, and Jewish Christian as well — asking for an appointment.

His reply: "Hectic schedule. Come six months from today."

During many long hours of prayer, the convert pondered what to ask during his interview. "I can't waste his time with abstractions and generalities." When the appointed day arrived, he walked into Father Simon's office, seated himself, and bluntly stated, "I have only one question: How do I become a saint?"

The Trappist's eyes narrowed; he leaned across the desk, took my friend's hand, and with fierce intensity whispered, "Will it!"

The interview was over.

Aware of the snares and pitfalls of Pelagianism, semi-Pelagianism, the bootstrap myth, the Horatio Alger legend of the self-made man, and do-it-yourself spirituality, I found Simon's answer addressing a real imbalance in my own interior life. Conscious that God takes the initiative and that by His grace we are saved, I am addressing the sincerity, seriousness, and ferocity of my determination to correspond with His saving grace. Apart from Him I can do nothing (see John 15:5). But without my cooperation, He can do nothing. Christ will not sanctify me against my will. I believe that He will finally give me exactly what

I choose and that the tendencies and desires my choices imply will be mine, irretrievably so. Obedience to the Word, the habit of constant prayer, and the daily practice of Christian virtue require active collaboration on my part. It means doing what Simon says: "Will it!"

The famous ballerina Martha Graham said the same thing from a different perspective:

> I am a dancer. I believe that we learn by practice. Whether it means to learn to dance by practicing dancing or to learn to live by practicing living, the principles are the same. In each it is the performance of a dedicated precise set of acts, physical or intellectual, from which comes the shape of achievement, a sense of one's being, a satisfaction of spirit. One becomes in some area an athlete of God. Practice means to perform, over and over again in the face of all obstacles, some act of vision, of faith, of desire. *Practice is a means of inviting the perfection desired.*[1]

Thomas Merton took up the same theme when he wrote, "You learn to pray by praying."

As I rambled down an old country road in the snowcapped hills of Pennsylvania, it struck me that Jesus addressed this question of grace and freedom in the mind-blowing parable of the farmer and the seed:

> This is how it is with the reign of God. A man scatters his seed on the ground. He goes to bed and gets up day after day. Through it all the seed sprouts and grows without his knowing how it happens. The soil produces of itself first the blade, then the ear, finally the ripe wheat in the

---

[1] Edward R. Murrow, ed., *This I Believe* (New York: Simon & Schuster, 1952).

ear. When the crop is ready, he wields the sickle, for the time is ripe for the harvest." He went on to say: "What comparison shall we use for the reign of God? It is like a mustard seed which, when planted in soil, is the smallest of all the earth's seeds, yet once it is sown, springs up to become the largest of shrubs, with branches big enough for the birds of the sky to build nests in its shade." By means of many such parables he taught them the message in a way they could understand. (Mark 4:26-33)

With serene confidence and sovereign authority Jesus explained, "The kingdom is not what you expected—a dazzling and dramatic intervention of unbearable glory. You see, it begins very small, tiny like a mustard seed. And it takes time to grow, so be patient."

Again Jesus said, "It's like a farmer who plants a seed and goes away, and later it sprouts." Ask any farmer in Pennsylvania or Vermont when he plants the wheat, and he will answer, "In late September or early October." Ask him what he does in the interim, and his surprised reply to your naïve question will be, "Nothin'! It grows by itself."

That's the way it is with the reign of God, Jesus explained. The kingdom will grow by itself. What the Father planted will be harvested, and nothing will get in the way. Not heresies, schisms, ecclesiastical blunders, defections, moral failures, not if the budget isn't balanced, not if I can't find a way to end this book, not persecutions or nuclear holocausts—nothing will obstruct the coming of the kingdom. That is certain. Human effort is as nothing compared to the inexorable plan of God.

What then of us weary apostles laboring in the vineyard and called to promote the kingdom of God? Do we just go back to bed? It would be wise to take another look at the prayer of Ignatius Loyola. Our Jesuit brothers have admitted to rewriting, reinterpreting, and putting glosses on it over the past four centuries. The prayer now reads: "Work as if everything depended on you and pray as if everything depended on God." That's right, isn't it? No! The original said, "Work as if everything depended on God and pray as if everything depended on you."

Did Ignatius write the original draft after he caught the startling meaning of the parable of the farmer and the seed? Regardless of the answer, I'm wondering what would happen in my life if I worked like everything depended on God and prayed like everything depended on me. I think I would be confident and carefree in ministry as never before, knowing that He is the primary agent, and I would pray with an unprecedented urgency and seriousness because the hastening of the kingdom pivoted on me. Oh, God, I would *will it* with all my heart and in the end prove Raphael Simon right—I would become a saint.

> As long as the readiness is there, a man is acceptable with whatever he can afford; never mind what is beyond his means. (2 Corinthians 8:12)

Lord, I want so much to do
BIG things for you.
I'd like so much
to make a grand gesture,
to do something
really spectacular.
Something BIG.

But you don't ask me
to do things like that.
You ask me to do
the little piddling things

that make up my everyday life.
You don't ask me
to do something
grand and glorious;
just to do my job.
You don't ask me
to do something really spectacular;
just to love my neighbor.
You don't ask me
to do something
absolutely stupendous;
just the routine,
day-in, day-out duties
of a working woman.

Lord, when I feel
that what I'm doing
is insignificant
and unimportant,
help me to remember
that everything I do
is significant
and important
in your eyes,
because you love me
and you put me here,
and no one else
can do
what I am doing
in exactly the way
I do it.

And, Lord,
I guess I'd better thank you
for not asking anything

tremendous of me.
When I think about it hard,
I don't really know
if I'd be up to it.

Thank you, Lord,
for knowing my capabilities.

CHAPTER 10

MIRACLE IN CHICAGO

*T*he headline in the San Jose Mercury trumpeted, "Fiancée Brings Him Back from the Dead." The date was July 12, 1978. The story unfolded in Chicago.

He wasn't supposed to live.

And even if he did, he wasn't ever supposed to move again. And even if he could move just a little — a finger or a toe — he wasn't supposed to walk again or talk again. He wasn't supposed to be normal again or do all the things a normal, strapping twenty-three-year-old man just out of the marines might do. Like take Linda, his fiancée, out dancing. Or dash out with her for pizza on Sunday afternoon. Or sit close to her on a Saturday night date. Or marry her — as he was planning before the accident.

But then the doctors and nurses didn't know Linda. And Linda made all the difference.

Peter Saraceno had been out to dinner with a buddy and was driving home. Suddenly, a truck cut him off. Peter jammed on the brakes of his mother's car, and it went into a spin. It headed for a light pole, rammed it down, and kept right on going. The car hit a huge electrical sign that buckled, then smashed down on the car, cutting it in two. The engine flew out of the hood. Peter flew out the door. He was thrown sixty-six feet and lay on the pavement — his head cracked wide open — when the medics arrived. The truck was nowhere in sight.

At Westlake Hospital in suburban Melrose Park, they pronounced Peter dead on arrival. But then the doctor felt for a pulse one last time and found one—very faint, but there.

"Three, four times they told us he had just a few hours left," said his mother, Louise Saraceno. "But I didn't believe it. And neither did Linda. They were engaged to be married. And Linda told me that before he died, she wanted to marry him. She wanted to be his wife."

Peter—strong, big, and still in good shape from the marines—did not die. But he lapsed into a coma. And every night Linda was at his side. Talking to him just as if it were any other night. As if they were on a date. As if nothing had happened.

After a month, Peter still didn't move or respond or flicker even an eyelash. Night after night, Linda came to the hospital from work and sat by his side. Toward late fall, after three and a half months, Peter came out of his coma. Slowly, moving only his eyes, he seemed to come back to life.

"His eyes followed Linda around the room," said one relative. Still he couldn't talk. He could barely move a finger. He lay there and looked at Linda. And Linda never let him down. On Halloween she put up decorations on the windows. On Christmas his room was filled with lighted trees. And on New Year's she celebrated with him alone. She filled the room with crepe paper and sixty-six balloons. "I had a cake and favors, and at midnight I put a hat on him and I blew horns and told him the New Year was here. The nurses thought I was crazy, but I figured he could hear me."

Slowly Peter began to recover. His movements came back: first in a finger, then an arm, then a leg. He began to try to talk. "I could only mumble," said Peter. "Nobody understood me but Linda. She knew everything I said. I could communicate through her."

Linda quit her job. She took special training to care for Peter. And she moved in with his widowed mother to help around the clock with Peter. With the money she'd saved up, she bought him an outdoor swimming pool so he could exercise his legs and work at his physical therapy.

"She wouldn't move from his side," said Mrs. Saraceno. "Without Linda, Peter never would have made it. She is something special—she is Peter's whole world."

A year later, Peter had begun to talk again. He worked hard at it until he could be understood. And then he asked the question he'd been waiting so long to ask: "Mr. Fraschalla, I'd like permission to marry your daughter."

"Peter," said Jim Fraschalla, "when you can walk down that aisle, she's all yours."

Peter couldn't walk then. He had to be carried. But slowly, cautiously, with the help of a walker, he began to walk again. And then one day he walked down the aisle with Linda.

Consciously or unconsciously (according to Matthew 25, it doesn't really matter), Linda Fraschalla plunged into the healing ministry of Jesus Christ. How? The story does not suggest that she ever laid hands on Peter, formally prayed over him, or anointed him with oil. Neither does the gospel say that Jesus ever did these things for Lazarus. "Where have you laid him?" He asked. "Lord, come and see," they said. Jesus began to weep, which caused the Jews to remark, "See how much He loved him!" Once again troubled in spirit, Jesus approached the tomb. It was a cave with a stone laid across it. "Take away the stone," Jesus directed. Then they took away the stone and Jesus looked upward and said, "Father, I thank You for having heard Me. I know that You always hear Me. But I have said this for the sake of the crowd, that they may believe that You sent Me." Having said this, He called loudly, "Lazarus, come out!" The dead man came out bound head and foot with linen strips, his face wrapped in a cloth. "Untie him," Jesus told them, "and let him go free" (see John 11:33-44).

The love in the heart of Jesus Christ restored His friend to life: "See how much He loved him!" With only a grateful acknowledgment to His heavenly Father for the sake of the crowd, Jesus acted. No mud or clay, oil or spittle, rosary, novena, or liturgical rite. Jesus' only resource was His own lonely heart. The healer is a lover.

Linda shared in that ministry through her presence, compassion, consolation, care, and comfort. *Comfort* means "strength together." Blessed are those who embrace each other in weakness because they will possess the land. When we take the great human risk of compassion, of suffering together, when we care to face the loneliness and pain of another, new life begins for both. Henri Nouwen wrote, "Comfort is the great human gift that creates community. Those who come together in mutual vulnerability are bound together by a new strength that makes them into one body."

As I read the story of Linda and her fiancé, I heard the voice of Mother Teresa. Asked by the British journalist Malcolm Muggeridge what her community tried to offer the dying, she replied,

> We want to make them feel that they are wanted, we want them to know that there are people who really love them, who really want them. . . . It is not very often *things* they need. What they need much more is what we offer them. In these twenty years of work amongst the people, I have come more and more to realize that it is being unwanted that is the worst disease that any human being can ever experience. Nowadays we have found medicine for leprosy and lepers can be cured. There's medicine for TB and consumptives can be cured. For all kinds of diseases there are medicines and cures. But for being unwanted, except there are willing hands to serve and there's a loving

heart to love, I don't think this terrible disease can ever be cured. (emphasis added)[1]

Could any surgical procedure, medicine, therapy, wonder drug, or prayer have saved Peter Saraceno without loving hands to make cakes and favors, to put up decorations, Christmas trees, crepe paper, and sixty-six balloons? Would Peter or Lazarus have lived if there had not been loving hearts to love them?

In my own ministry to others, the greatest percentage of time is devoted to healing through caring. Often people request prayers for deliverance, inner healing, or physical healing. But more frequently they simply want a man or woman to whom they can turn — not because of what this person is able to do but because of what he or she is: a person who makes them feel wanted, a friend to love them, one who generates an atmosphere of warmth and trust in which they are able to love in return.

Several years ago in Atlantic City, New Jersey, Francis MacNutt shared in a personal testimony his introduction to the charismatic renewal. After receiving the baptism of the Holy Spirit at a Camps Farthest Out meeting, he prayed for discernment with a group of elders as to what his role in the Catholic Church should be. Francis's mind raced. (I'm paraphrasing this badly.) A prophet? A healer like the late Kathryn Kuhlmann? A Catholic Billy Graham evangelizing the world? Perhaps God had something even more grandiose in mind: apostolic leadership — bishop, cardinal?

"I can't tell you how disappointed I was," Francis said, "when the communal discernment disclosed that my role in the church was to be a loving man! That's all?"

Yes, that was all. And the most powerful healing ministry in the American Catholic Church matured because a healer is a lover.

---

[1] Malcolm Muggeridge, *Something Beautiful for God* (New York: Harper & Row, 1971), 91–92.

Finally, there is a ministry to God Himself. Bizarre as it sounds, the ministry of praising God's goodness, wisdom, and love during times of pain and heartache is a beautiful expression of faith in action, a living expression of trust that "God makes *all* things work together for the good of those who have been called according to his decree" (Romans 8:28, emphasis added). In his moving little book *Our Heavenly Father,* Dr. Robert Frost wrote,

> There is nothing more precious to God than our praise during affliction. Not praise for what the devil has done, but praise for the redeeming power of our loving heavenly Father. What He does not protect us from, He will perfect us through. There is indeed a special blessing for those who do not become offended in God during adversity. Furthermore, we become a special blessing to Him![2]

Let me share a second example of ministering to the Lord in the moment of *His* adversity. Ironically this happened in Chicago's South Side on Holy Thursday night. I wrote in my journal,

> The adoration of the Lord Jesus in the Eucharist began with a heaviness within me. It's freezing outside; the chapel is cold; my mind is opaque; but foremost is the nagging doubt about my own sincerity. Earlier in the day I sensed a residual resistance, a tug in the direction of nonacceptance, when I read, "Where the Spirit of the Lord is, there is freedom." Do I really want to be free? Do I honestly desire a kingdom lifestyle? What are the *real* tendencies and desires of my heart? Do I long more than anything else to be God's man? Difficult and demanding as it is, do I truly prefer to renounce rather than receive

[2] Robert Frost, *Our Heavenly Father* (Plainfield, NJ: Logos International, 1978), 135–136.

much of what life has to offer? To serve rather than be served? To pray when I could play? Be slow to speak, Brennan, be cautious to answer. . . . I felt confusion and discouragement tiding within me.

Then a beautiful thing happened. Like a flash of lightning illuminating my mind, I realized that the only reason I was at prayer was because I wanted to be with my Friend. The doubt and uncertainty vanished. I knew I wanted to comfort Jesus in His loneliness and fear in the garden. I wanted to reach out, touch Him, and take Him in my arms. I wanted to watch not an hour but the whole night with Him. The only words that formed on my lips were those of the little boy Willie-Juan in the fairy tale I had written the year past. Over and over I whispered, "I love You, my Friend."

With the quiet reassurance that faith gives, I knew that I was utterly sincere. I asked Jesus to look over at me and know that I was there. "You were the One who taught me that a friend is someone who is present not only to laugh with you when you are happy but who *stays* when you are lonely, sad, hurting, and rejected. I thank You with all my heart for the gift of being able to really care for the courage to stand by You in the loneliness of Your Passion, to believe that in my brokenness and fickleness I really do love You.

What do I have that I have not received? Tonight if I boast, I shall boast about what You have done in my life. I love You, my Friend. All I want is You, Senor; all I want is You.

Lord, it ought to be easy to talk to you
any time,
any place.
But often I find it difficult.
There are so many busy things to do;
so many interruptions,
so many worrisome things that distract me.
And generally, just when I think
the time is right
and everything is under control,
someone talks at me.
There are so many people, Lord,
who talk at me.
And so many of them annoy me.
So many of them talk and talk,
and say nothing.
And yet, Lord,
somebody's got to listen sometime.

People talked at you, too,
and I can't find a single place
in the Bible
that says you didn't stop
to listen.
You must've been impatient sometimes,
tired and hungry,
worn from walking and from teaching,
wanting to be alone for a little while
so you could talk to your Father.
But You listened
because somebody has to listen.
You listened,
and they went away
comforted, healed and helped.

Forgive me, Lord, for my impatience
with your other children.
For my annoyance, my boredom,
and even, sometimes, Lord, my anger.
Forgive me for my selfishness
that makes me think my own words
to you
are more important than
another's need.

Let me learn to listen, Lord,
not just with my ears
but with my heart.

And once the listening's done,
I know you will provide
the quiet and calm I need
to raise my voice
in praise of you.

CHAPTER 11

REALLY HUMAN —
REALLY POOR

*L*ast year at the end of a parish week of renewal in Louisiana, a man approached me outside the rectory, muttered "I've prayed about this," slipped an envelope into my pocket, and hurried away. I was overdue at a reception in the parish hall, so I jogged over there, completely forgetting about the envelope. Preparing for bed later that night, I cleaned out my pockets, opened the envelope, and looked at a check for six thousand dollars for God's poor.

The next day I sent the money off to a poor man with a large family in desperate financial straits. Know what happened? Within five days I received nine letters overflowing with gratitude from the man, describing in detail how the money was being used to help his family and others. That experience gave me a beautiful insight into what a poor man is like.

When he receives a gift, he experiences and expresses genuine gratitude. Having nothing, he appreciates even a slight gift. I have been given the utterly undeserved gift of salvation in Jesus Christ. Through no merit of mine but by His mercy, I've been given a bona fide invitation to drink new wine forever at the wedding feast in the kingdom of God. The psalmist said, "The Lord has prepared a feast for me; given wine in plenty for me to drink" (23:5). Jesus promised, "I will give you the kingdom that my Father gave to me, and in that kingdom you will eat and drink at my table" (Luke 22:29-30).

For an alcoholic, that's heaven.

The more a man realizes that he has received a gift he can never repay, he "notifies his face" and the tenor of his life becomes one of humble, joyful thanksgiving. He simply rejoices in the gift and writes nine letters to Yahweh that cry out, "Give thanks to the LORD for He is good, his kindness endures forever" (Psalm 107:1).

Is this why Francis of Assisi is so universally loved and why Pope Benedict XV called him "the most perfect image of Christ that ever was"? G. K. Chesterton once remarked that Henry Cardinal Newman wrote a book called *Grammar of Assent*. It could be said that Francis wrote *Grammar of Gratitude*.

Francis's sense of thanksgiving and utter dependence on God were not sentiment but reality, not fancy but fact. He understood, down to its very depths, the theory of thanks—and its depths were a bottomless abyss. The little poor man concerned himself chiefly with the highest kind of giving, which is thanksgiving. He knew himself to be a man possessed totally by another, belonging totally to another, and dependent totally on another.

One day when the brothers were discussing which virtue does more to make a close friend of Christ, Francis, as though making known to them a secret of his heart, answered, "Know, my sons, that poverty is the special way to salvation; its fruits are manifold, but it is really well known only to a few."[1]

The Sermon on the Mount is a portrait of the heart of Jesus Christ. The Beatitudes offer a deep insight into His preferences, prejudices, and total personality. In giving us what John Powell called the BE-ATTITUDES, Jesus said that these are the attitudes that will enable you to *be* like Him. He talked about *being* pure of heart. He talked about *being* compassionate. He talked about the attitudes that are deep down inside us, and He

---

[1] Thomas of Celano, *Francis Trilogy* (Hyde Park, NY: New City Press, 2004), 200.

said, "If you really want to be like Me, this is how you ought to think." And right atop the list is "Be poor in spirit."

How dearly Jesus loves the poor in spirit. St. Thérèse of Lisieux, known as the Little Flower, put it this way: "The poorer you are, the more Jesus will love you."

To be poor in spirit means to cling to your impoverished humanity and to have nothing to brag about before God. Paul wrote, "What do you have that you haven't received; and if you have received it, why do you go about boasting as if you hadn't received it?"

The poverty of Jesus' spirit is captured beautifully in His spontaneous reply to the rich young man: "Why do you call me good? No one is good but God alone" (Matthew 19:17). This inner attitude of Jesus ravished the heart of His Father: "I solemnly assure you, the Son cannot do anything by himself—he can only do what he sees the Father doing" (John 5:19). Jesus acknowledged that everything is a loving gift from the Father's hand. And He cried out, "How pleasing you are in my Father's eyes when you have this be-attitude, this attitude of being poor like Me, when you accept the limits of your humanity." This is the basic attitude for admission to the kingdom.

Of course, the Evil One gets upset when we cling to our humanness. He was very distressed in the desert with Jesus for this very reason. He wanted Jesus to renounce His poverty, His humanness. Satan already knew that when Jesus accepted the poverty of the human condition, the saga of salvation history was moving toward its climax. And Jesus held nothing back, clung to nothing, permitted nothing to shield Him—even His true origin. "He did not deem equality with God something to be grasped. Rather he emptied himself" (Philippians 2:6-7). And Satan was furious.

Theologian Johannes Metz offered deep insight into why being truly human means becoming truly poor:

Satan, however, tries to obstruct this self-renunciation, this thoroughgoing "poverty." Satan wants to make Jesus strong, for what the devil really fears is the powerlessness of God in the humanity Christ has assumed. Satan fears the trojan horse of an open human heart that will remain true to its native poverty, suffer the misery and abandonment that is humanity's, and thus save humankind. Satan's temptation is an assault on God's self-renunciation, an enticement to strength, security and spiritual abundance; for these things will obstruct God's saving approach to humanity in the dark robes of frailty and weakness.[2]

All of Satan's temptations to Jesus were to *spiritualism*. First, he tried to appeal to the divinity in Jesus. (As a matter of fact, Satan always tries to stress our spiritual strength, our divine character. He has done this from the very beginning. "You will be like God" is the slogan of the Evil One. It is *the* temptation he sets before us in countless variations, urging us to reject the truth of the humanity we have been given.)

How true in my own life! Every time that I try to soar above the inherent limitations of my human nature and pretend I'm an *angel*, I wind up playing the *beast*. Alcoholism is a good example—a futile attempt to escape the poverty, loneliness, and frustration that are so much a part of the human condition. The same may be said of the drug culture. The name of the game doesn't change. Intellectual pride fits into this category. I attempt to bridge the vast gulf that separates creature from Creator by disavowing my limited finite intelligence and take myself so seriously that I feel superior to others. I presume that I am more important in the eyes of God than the brother who cooks in the kitchen.

---

[2] Johannes Baptist Metz, *Poverty of Spirit*, trans. John Drury (Mahwah, NJ: Paulist, 1968), 10–11.

Insidiously, Satan stresses my charismatic gifts and ensnares me in spiritualism.

Several years ago in the middle of a weekend retreat, I inquired, "How did the Yankees do yesterday?" (It was World Series Week.) "I wouldn't know and I couldn't care," answered one brother with a condescending air of angelic contempt. *Beware of the spiritualists.*

Metz continued,

> The temptation in the desert would have Jesus betray humanity in the name of God. . . . Jesus' "no" to Satan is His "yes" to our poverty. He did not cling to his divinity. He did not simply dip into our existence, wave a magic wand of divine life over us and then hurriedly retreat back to his eternal home. Nor did he leave us with a tattered dream, letting us brood over the mystery of our existence. . . .
>
> With the full weight of his divinity he descended into the abyss of human existence, penetrating its darkest depths. He was not spared from the dark mystery of our poverty as human beings.[3]

He tasted failure, sorrow, loneliness, and brokenness.

Here was a man, Hebrews says, "tempted as we are, yet without sinning" (4:15). Sin does not magnify the suffering of man's plight; instead, it mitigates it. When I sin, I seek an escape from my humanity. I used to say to myself, "Well, you're only human!" But sin does not make me human; it compromises my humanity. The philandering husband with his mistress on business trips, the chemically addicted, the thieves who build ivory towers out of stolen money, the sensation-seekers and power brokers who seek substitutes. They do not drink the poverty of the human

---

[3] Metz, 12.

situation down to the last drop. They dare not stare it full in the face. The sins of my past represent my own secret compromise with the forces of loneliness, frustration, suffering, and death. I join forces with them before they can assault me and make me truly poor.

Metz continued,

> Have we really understood the impoverishment that Christ endured? Everything was taken from him during the passion, even the love that drove him to the cross. No longer did he savor his own love, no longer did he feel any spark of enthusiasm. His heart gave out and a feeling of utter helplessness came over him. Truly he emptied himself (Phil. 2:7). God's merciful hand no longer sustained him. God's countenance was hidden during the passion.[4]

Jesus did not die a death with dignity but a death endured, screaming to a God who did not answer. Jesus paid the price. He became utterly poor. In this total renunciation, Jesus professed what it means to be human. He endured our lot. He came to us where we really were and stood with us, struggling with His whole heart to have us say yes to our innate poverty.

The Christian who is really human is really poor. How does this poverty of spiritism reflect itself in day-to-day living?

In conversation, the poor man always leaves the other person with the feeling, "My life has been enriched by talking with you." And it has. He is not all exhaust and no intake. He doesn't impose himself on another; he doesn't overwhelm him with his wealth of insights; he doesn't try to convert him by concussion with one sledgehammer blow of the Bible after another. He listens well because he realizes he is poor and has so much to learn from others. His poverty enables him to enter the existential world of

---

[4] Metz, 13.

the other, even when he cannot identify with that world. Being poor, he knows how to receive and can express appreciation and gratitude for the slightest gift.

Peter van Breeman, S. J., has written that the poor man accepts himself. He has a self-image in which the awareness of his limitation is very vivid but that does not depress him. This consciousness of his own insufficiency without feelings of self-hatred is typical of the poor in spirit.[5]

He realizes that he does not love as much as his heart would wish. This past Lent, I preached six week-long parish renewals in succession. The last one was in Downers Grove, Illinois, and on closing night I was pretty wiped out. More than one thousand people had attended, and as the recessional song began, I debated whether my body could handle another half hour of farewells and blessings in the vestibule. I could flee to the sacristy, divest, run to my room, and crash. Spirit willing but flesh rebelling. Finally, I prayed for a little zap, opted for the vestibule, got into it as best I could, and hit the boards around eleven.

The next morning a note addressed to me lay on the breakfast table. It read, "Dear Father Manning, I attended your parish renewal all this week. You are eloquent, brilliant, witty, poetic, aesthetic and . . . *inflated*. Last night when you stood in the vestibule after the service ended, where was the love in your eyes for each of us in the midst of your glory? Why didn't you stoop down and hug those little children? Why didn't you kiss the old ladies on the cheek? Why didn't you look at us with your eyes from the core of your being, depth meeting depth, love meeting love? Man, are you blind!" The letter was signed, "A mirror."

Obviously the woman needed something that I didn't give. Under the circumstances her expectations may have been unreasonable. But even when I'm not tired, I realize that I don't love as

---

[5] See Peter G. van Breeman, *As Bread That Is Broken* (Denville, NJ: Dimension Books, 1974), 116.

much as I could or should. Lots of times I think of a thoughtful thing to say twenty minutes after the person has walked out the door. I miss cues. Sometimes I hear what a woman says but not what she means and wind up giving sage counsel to a nonproblem.

Distracted after a disturbing phone call, I left the monastery to give a talk to the inmates of Trenton State Prison and began with the outrageous greeting, "Well, it's nice to see so many of you here!" And so it goes. Frequently not in form, on top, or in control. That is part of my poverty as a human being, and self-acceptance without self-concern simply expresses a reality. An impoverished spirit prevents the poor man from being a tyrant to himself.

If you asked the poor man to describe his prayer life, he might well answer, "Most of the time my prayer consists of experiencing the absence of God in the hope of communion." He is not richly endowed with extraordinary graces and mystical experience. Yet the experience of absence does not mean the absence of experience. Like the soldier in combat sneaking a look at his wife's picture tucked in his helmet, the experience of her absence does not mean at that moment the absence of an experience of her. And somehow the poor man perceives that religious experience is not the goal of the spiritual life but union with God through love. With singer Joe Wise, the Christian who is really human and really poor goes to the table of the Lord singing, "Poor though we are, we have brought ourselves to you: we are yours, we are yours."

Jesus, my Brother and Lord, I pray as I write these words for the grace to be truly poor before You, to recognize and accept my weakness and humanness, to forego the indecent luxury of self-hatred, to celebrate Your mercy and trust in Your power when I'm at my weakest, to rely on Your love no matter what I may do, to seek no escapes from my innate poverty, to accept loneliness when it comes instead of seeking substitutes, to live peacefully without clarity or assurance, to stop grandstanding and trying to get attention, to do the truth quietly without display, to let the dishonesties in my life fade away, to belong no more to myself, not to desert my post when I give the appearance of staying at it, to cling to my humanity, to accept the limitations and full responsibility of being a human being—really human and really poor in Christ our Lord.

Lord, I think maybe
you're getting me
accustomed
to the idea
that I'm not
an archangel.

Of course,
you know I'm not
and I know I'm not.
But I must admit
that periodically
I try to behave
as though I were.
And most of my problems
seem to stem
directly
from that fact.

I'd like to think
I'm perfect;
with no limitations,
impure motives,
human weaknesses;
everything
under control

and
all together.
And every time
I catch myself
thinking
and behaving
that way
life becomes
not just burdensome
but horrendous.

Lord, thank you
for letting me know
that I'm not perfect
yet
but that you'll get me there
if I let you.
Thank you
for reminding me
that I'll never have it
all together
until we meet
face to face.

Lord, do archangels
need you
as much as I do?

Father, thank you
for setting me free.
Free to be
poor,
little,
weak.

Thank you
for setting me free.
Free to be
misunderstood,
rejected,
forgotten.

Thank you
for setting me free.
Free to be
unsatisfied,
empty,
stripped.

Thank you
for setting me free.
Free to
break through,
let go,
enter the flame.

Father, thank you
for setting me free
by binding me
more closely
to yourself.

CHAPTER 12

THE FRIARS

((There are a great many people who get upset at the death of a great man. I have to admit that I used to be one of those people, but no more. He has left so many great memories that it makes one feel rather good whenever his name is mentioned. You don't have time to remember any of the bad things that happened to you if you remember the good things he left."

These words were spoken of the late John F. Kennedy by the legendary basketball star Maurice Stokes; little did Stokes know that he was writing his own epitaph. A graduate of my alma mater, St. Francis College in Loretto, Pennsylvania, Stokes died in the fall of 1969. After eleven years of paralysis during which time he couldn't walk, Stokes was afflicted three months before his death with spinal meningitis, diphtheria, and a punctured lung that finally caused his heart to stop. A few minutes before he died, he asked to be buried on the campus of St. Francis College because, he said, "It was there that I found God and the meaning of friendship."

At a twilight funeral Mass at the college (founded by my own Third Order Regular community in 1847 and still operating under us), nine hundred students with torchlights met the casket at the chapel door after the Eucharistic liturgy and accompanied it to the graveyard, where only Franciscan friars are interred. As Stokes' body was lowered into the earth, the community of priests, brothers, family, friends, faculty, and students sang the blessing of St. Francis: "The Lord bless you and keep you; may He show His face to you and have mercy; may He turn His countenance to you and give you peace."

During the eulogy he preached at Mass, the president of the college, Father Vincent Negherbon, T. O. R., said,

> The community of St. Francis College bows its head in sadness at the death of our beloved alumnus Maurice Stokes. Rarely has a college had cause to be as proud of one of its sons as we have of Maurice. His extraordinary skill, his indomitable courage, his deathless spirit will live on in Loretto as long as there is a community known as St. Francis College.

Stokes, called one of the greatest basketball players in the history of the sport, led obscure, unheralded St. Francis to national recognition and was voted the most valuable player in the National Invitational Tourney in 1953 and 1954. His family said that the Mass and burial service had inestimable meaning for them and their relatives and friends who gathered in Loretto.

Thirty priests concelebrated the liturgy. I was there doing nothing, saying little, just immensely proud to be a priest of the Third Order Regular of St. Francis of Penance. It is an honor to wear this black habit with the capuche and white cord. I do not and cannot maintain that we are a community of saints and scholars for the simple reason that many of you know me personally. There are blemishes, flaws, and character defects in every friar. On a community level we have not always been prayerful. Our educational institutions are not always what they should be. Often we have not been a community of prophets portraying to the students the vision of radical gospel living because we've gotten bogged down in our own personal fears and insecurities, in organizational dilemmas and the budget. In my five years of college teaching, I frequently failed to communicate to others a passion for truth, love, and the person of Jesus Christ because I didn't have it myself.

I consider myself a typical friar—a poor, *weak*, sinful man with hereditary faults and limited talents, trying (with a little help from my friends) to live the gospel.

For a moment I wish to explore the idea of weakness because it has opened up a new depth of self-understanding and community awareness.

With considerable perception Father Michael Buckley has observed that there is a practice among Americans, common and obvious enough, when estimating a man's aptitude for a profession and a career: You list his strengths. Peter is a good speaker, possesses an able mind, exhibits genuine talent for leadership and debate; he would make an excellent lawyer. Steve has good judgment, a scientific bent, obvious manual dexterity, and human concerns; he would make a splendid surgeon.

Now the tendency is to transfer this method of evaluation to the priesthood, to line up all the pluses—socially adept, intellectually perceptive, characterized by interior integrity, sound common sense, and habits of prayer—and to judge that such a man would make a fine priest.

Buckley wrote,

> I think this transfer is disastrous. There is a further pressing question, one proper to the priesthood, if not uniquely proper to it: Is this man *weak* enough to be a priest? Let me spell out what I mean. Is this man deficient enough so that he can't ward off significant suffering from his life, so that he lives with a certain amount of failure, so that he feels what it is to be an average man?

By the way, I believe that this applies to *every follower of Christ* because we are a "priesthood of all believers" (see 1 Peter 2:9).

It is in this deficiency, in this interior lack, in this *weakness*, maintains the book of Hebrews, that the efficacy of the ministry and priesthood of Christ lies.

For because he himself has suffered and been tempted,
he is able to help those who are tempted. . . . For we
do not have a high priest who is unable to sympathize
with our weaknesses, but one who in every respect has
been tempted as we are, but without sinning. . . . He can
deal gently with the wayward and the ignorant, since he
himself is beset with weakness. (4:14-16)

As often as I have read this passage, my mind still reels when
I think that the inspired author of Hebrews easily acknowledged
that our High Priest, the Son of the living God, was beset with
weakness! Confronted with this fait accompli, how terribly important it is for Christians to enter into the seriousness of this revelation, of this conjunction between priesthood and weakness, that
we dwell upon deficiency as part of our vocation. Otherwise we
can secularize our lives into an amalgam of desires and talents,
and we can feel our weakness as a threat to our priesthood, as
indicative that we should rethink, as symptomatic that we were
never genuinely called, that the resources are not ours to complete
what we once thought was our destiny and which spoke to our
generosity and fidelity. (God, how I wrestled with this as I stum-
bled down the road to alcoholic oblivion . . .)

What do I mean by *weakness*? Not the experience of sin,
though weakness may be the context from which sin arises, but
the experience of a peculiar liability to suffering. A profound sense
of inability, both to do and to protect; an inability, even after great
effort, to author, perform, effect what we have wanted, or with the
success we would have wanted; to try to craft *Souvenirs of Solitude*
into a spiritual masterpiece already knowing that because of my
inherent limitations there are frontiers I cannot cross, depths I
cannot plumb, heights I cannot climb, horizons beyond my vision;
an inability to secure my own future, to protect myself, to live
with clarity and assurance, or to ward off shame and suffering.

If a man is clever enough, devious enough, or poised enough,
he can limit his expectations and accomplish pretty much what he

would want. He can secure his perimeters and live without a sense of failure or inadequacy or shame before what might have been. But if you can't — either because of your history or your temperament or your situation — then you experience failure at the heart of your life. And this experience, rather than militating against your priesthood, is part of its essential structure.

How paradoxical this mystery is: The strength of the priesthood lies precisely in and through the weakness of our humanity. Why? For two reasons, I think. Weakness relates us profoundly to the people we serve; it allows us to feel with them the human condition, the human struggle and darkness and anguish that call out for salvation. Further, weakness relates us profoundly and apostolically to God because it provides the arena in which His power can move and reveal itself; His power is made manifest in weakness.

And so Paul cried, "I will all the more gladly glory in my weakness, that the power of Christ may rest upon me. For the sake of Christ, then, I am content with weaknesses, insults, hardships, persecutions and calamities; for when I am weak, then I am strong" (2 Corinthians 12:9-10).

There is a collective consequence that follows from all this. Our Christian communities must make such a life possible; we must support one another in weakness, forgiving one another's daily faults and carrying one another's burdens. It is absurd to maintain weakness as part of the priestly vocation and the spiritual life and then to belittle those who are weak, resent those who are insensitive and clumsy, allow disagreements to become hostilities, or continue battles and angers because of personal feelings.

The commandment and judgment on our lives is that we should love one another as He loved us — as He cared, out of His weakness, for our weakness. This is the foundation of our lives together, the deep mystery of our mutual presence in Christ Jesus, and an urgent summons always to be reconciled to one another.

But words are brave; deeds are difficult. If I am the typical friar, I have failed in this more times than I can remember. Yet there is something I shall never forget. In the years since I returned from an alcoholic rehabilitation center in Hazelden, no mention has ever been made in the community that I was a drunk. Moreover, there have been no patronizing or condescending airs; no threats, cautions, admonitions, or limits placed on my life or ministry; not a trace of anxious concern over a relapse.

There is a story told of St. Margaret of Cortona, the Mary Magdalen of the Franciscans. She forsook a life of public sin, turned to prayer and penance, and eventually became a canonized saint. One evening while at prayer in a small chapel in Assisi, a Franciscan brother approached her and abruptly ordered her out of the chapel: "It's 6 p.m., and I'm locking up." Margaret withdrew humbly, but she was piqued.

Later that night while talking with our Lord, she complained about the brother's discourtesy and tossed in a few other complaints she had about the friars. The Lord listened patiently. When Margaret ended her harangue, He said quietly, "My little one, all the things you say of the friars are true and then some, but I cannot become angry with them."

"Why, Lord?" Margaret asked.

"Because they do one thing that makes up for all their faults. They are kind to sinners."

It is not a perfect community, and the need for ongoing renewal continues. But these are the men of whom the late Maurice Stokes said, "They led me to God and taught me the meaning of friendship." Honorable men — it's been a privilege to live with them.

> My thoughts are not your thoughts, my ways not your ways — it is Yahweh who speaks. Yes, the heavens are as high above earth as my ways are above your ways, my thoughts above your thoughts. (Isaiah 55:8-9)

Lord, the nicest thing about you
is that you always
think better of us
than we think of ourselves.
That you always
have more confidence in us
than we have in ourselves.
That you always
find us more attractive
than we find ourselves.
That you always
expect more of us
than we expect of ourselves.
That you always
know us better
than we know ourselves.
That you always
forgive us
before we can ever
forgive ourselves.
That you always
accept us as we are
before we can ever
accept ourselves.
That you always
love us more
than we can ever
love ourselves.

Thank you, Lord,
for being you.

CHAPTER 13

GOOD HUMOR

When the late Katherine Granahan was treasurer of the United States during the Kennedy era, she came to our seminary in Loretto to speak on pornography and censorship. When asked by a canonist to define pornography, this ebullient lady replied, "I can't define it, but I know it when I see it!"

Good humor is one of those qualities more easily sensed than defined. Like so many exquisite things — the beauty of a Beethoven symphony, the strength of a Van Gogh painting, the charm of a well-bred person — good humor is as elusive as it is real. It might be defined negatively as the elimination of everything that offends, saddens, or worries others; the elimination of every disorder, defect, and mannerism that makes life harder and more annoying for others — sulkiness, affectation, moodiness, vain prattling, stubborn insistence, obnoxious backslapping. My former girlfriend Barbara once told me, "Man, your table manners are gross!" That kind of stuff.

Positively, good humor might be defined as unaffected graciousness, sincere friendliness. It is serene, soothing, straightforward, and affable. It makes us want to take pains to be pleasing to others and to avoid the slipshod manners that many of us adopt among our intimate friends. Inwardly, good humor is a disposition to gracious service, a capacity to look upon others, regardless of their origins, as God's children and friends.

Effectiveness in the ministry is enhanced by good humor. Remember the prayer of Teresa of Ávila: "From silly devotions and sour-faced saints, spare us, O Lord"? Good humor is not a super-ficial smile, a grin-and-bear-it attitude, or the "ginger peachy" mentality. It is rooted securely in the faith conviction that *I am loved by God as I am, not as I should be.* This disposition invites others to love and admire the gospel style of life. A good-humored Christian who accepts others as they are, not as they should be, is an evangelist. A zealous but ill-humored evangelist can cause others to say, "If that's what religion does to you, sit on it."

One wintry day shortly before I was ordained, I was sliding down an icy hill in Loretto on the way to class. The road was a sheet of sleet and snow, and the wind whipped through my clothes. Icicles had formed on my eyebrows, and my face was twisted in an archipelago-style grimace. I did not look or feel like I was saved.

My companion was seventy-year-old Swiss-born Father Anton Feyer, who taught Hebrew, Greek, church history, and whatever else was needed at the seminary. Icicles had formed on his bushy eyebrows too, but his face was bright with laughter as if in the midst of a game he thoroughly enjoyed. His eyes twinkled, his jowls and tummy bobbed up and down, and a mischievous smile played at the corners of his mouth. He looked like Santa Claus leaving the North Pole on Christmas Eve. Annoyed, I asked, "What makes you so happy, Father Feyer?" He looked at me and in his thick German accent answered, "Brudder Brennan, I am a member of a redeemed community!" The conscious awareness of his real identity and his membership in the community of God's people generated a warmth and affability that the frost and ice could not penetrate.

Through good humor a Christian triumphs over that subtle form of egotism that would make him pose as a martyr or at least a victim, that makes him want to be noticed, consoled, or placed on a pedestal. And it makes community life richer and more delightful.

Paul called good humor a charism and exhorted the Christian community at Philippi to manifest it:

Rejoice in the Lord always! Rejoice! Everyone should see how unselfish you are. The Lord is near. Dismiss all anxiety from your minds. Present your needs to God in every form of prayer and in petitions full of gratitude. Then God's own peace, which is beyond all understanding, will stand guard over your hearts and minds, in Christ Jesus. (Philippians 4:4-7)

After an interview with someone, Abraham Lincoln remarked to his secretary, "I don't like that man's face."

She reacted in amazement, "But that's what his face is; he's not responsible for his face."

And Lincoln replied tartly, "After forty every man is responsible for his face."

My face is the mirror of my moods. After four decades of dying and rising, I should have acquired sufficient emotional maturity to master my moods and maintain a tranquil facial expression. I think that's what Honest Abe was implying.

I would not be writing this little chapter if a woman had not asked me this morning, "Why are you in such a rotten mood?"

For the sorrowing every day is evil,
    for the joyous heart it is festival always. (Proverbs 15:15)

Lord, thank you
for the gift of laughter.
For the boisterous laughter
of small boys
as they wade ankle-deep in muddy water.
For the helpless giggles
of little girls,

clustered together like a bunch of daisies.
For the fat chuckle
of a sleepy baby.
For the loud guffaws
of a crowd of teenage boys.
For the silver ripple
of a young girl's laugh.
For the sweet, wise smiles
of the very old.
For the soft, shared laughter
of lovers everywhere.

Thank you, Lord,
for this gift of laughter.

CHAPTER 14

EVANGELIZATION

*((C*hristianity will go. It will shrink and vanish. I needn't argue about that; I'm right, and I will be proved right. We're more popular than Jesus now; I don't know which will go first—rock 'n' roll or Christianity."

This quote is from an article written many years ago by the late John Lennon, member of and lyric writer for the Beatles. The day after the article appeared, the Beatles were greeted at a London airport by ten thousand worshippers shouting, "John, yes! Jesus, no!" Thousands of Americans resented the sacrilegious nature of Lennon's remark and began a Ban-the-Beatles campaign. But the most perceptive observation on the matter was made by Thurston Davis, the late editor of the Jesuit weekly *America*: "It seems to me that Lennon was simply stating what many a Christian educator would admit—that Christianity must come alive again in the hearts of the young."

On August 23, 1978, the following article appeared in the St. Petersburg, Florida, *Times*: "The students knew immediately that the Beatles were associated with *A Hard Day's Night*," said Dr. Arthur M. Sanderson. "But less than a third attributed the Sermon on the Mount to Christ."

Dr. Sanderson is a professor at the University of South Florida, Tampa, and head of the journalism division, department of mass communication. Not long ago he gave his Beginnings Reporting Class a list of one hundred classical works—paintings, books, music, inventions—and asked them to name the creators.

"The results," said Sanderson, "were absolutely dismal. The average score was about 20 right of the 100 questions." Sanderson's conclusion: Reading, writing, speaking, and listening have settled into listening with today's young people, but what they are listening to and watching are the latest rock albums, *Kojak*, and *The Bionic Woman*.

John Lennon's forecast was ominous. Since then, participation in Sunday Mass has decreased to 27 percent. Enrollment in seminaries has dropped drastically. Sacramental involvement on every level has diminished, and the divorce rate in the Christian community has soared to a stunning 51 percent.

The Fathers of Vatican II, speaking of the mission of the church in the Decree on the Lay Apostolate, said: "The first task is that of evangelization and sanctification, of bringing people to conscious faith in Jesus Christ. Second is the work of renewing the temporal order, and third the works of charity and the corporal works of mercy." The late Paul VI issued a clarion call to make evangelization the universal church's top priority, and the same theme has been echoed by the American hierarchy in meetings of the National Council of Catholic Bishops. Sadly, this call has not been heeded.

The fundamental mission of the church is preaching the Good News of Jesus Christ. But there has been a loss of faith in the power of the Word. We feel it won't be effective if we say it like it is. It will turn people off. Let's rebuild the temporal order first.

But there is a startling discontinuity between human reasoning and what God's Word says the priority is. War, loneliness, world hunger, abortion are rooted in man's rebellion. Man must submit in faith to Jesus Christ and repent. Putting a band-aid here and there on this or that moral problem is not the answer. Evangelization hits the core—man must submit in faith to Jesus Christ and repent. He must renounce his autonomy and self-sufficiency. Personal appropriation of the death and resurrection of Christ is the one foundation for Christian community and world peace.

Failure to act on the gospel imperative to evangelize has resulted in holding to the form of Christianity while denying its power. Beautiful liturgies; mass regional, national, and international meetings; crusades against immorality are good and have their place, but none of them is an adequate substitute for dying to self. Explicit commitment to the person of Jesus Christ is the essence of the evangelical message. When He is not explicitly the center, what results is confusion about the mission of the church. The battle cry becomes "Get involved in the issues of the time. Don't be an ostrich. Be relevant. Give witness." But if the root problem of cosmic, world, and personal evil is man's rebelliousness, if the radical solution cannot be had without conversion to Jesus Christ, then the mission of the church is preaching the gospel to all creatures, inviting them to repent and find salvation.

Studies like Sanderson's underscore the importance of listening in our culture. Obviously the primary medium of evangelization is the proclamation of the Word through prime-time television, radio, recordings. However, Sanderson also emphasized the paramount importance of the quality of the presentation. *A Hard Day's Night* was quickly identified because the Beatles' lyrics, beat, and presence spoke to the Now generation.

My own experience, as well as that of many other evangelists, verifies that you can tell it like it is, that the majority of people are turned off, but that the Word will not return empty. Father John Bertolucci went to a wedding reception and ended up evangelizing six hundred people. In Marrero, Louisiana, during a parish renewal, I was asked to speak to three hundred high school girls. For them it was a command performance. Most didn't want to be there. They came to the church giddy, chattering, laughing, and starving for lunch at noon. I planned to speak for one hour on the theme "Jesus Christ Crucified: The Power of God and the Wisdom of God." I never finished. After forty minutes the sobbing was so loud I had to stop. I invited the girls to come forward and venerate the cross as we do on Good Friday. The movement from their seats to the sanctuary represented a movement away from the darkness in their lives to the light who is Jesus Christ, a conversion, a turning from self-centeredness to the Man who loved them and delivered Himself up for them. "But for Christ's sake," I pleaded, "don't come up here if you're playing a game. Come back tomorrow, or next year, or twenty years from now, but don't make a mockery of the greatest Lover the world has ever known. We've got too many phonies and fakers in the church already honoring Jesus with their lips and denying Him by their lifestyle."

We then listened as the monks of Weston Priory recited from Hosea: "Come back to me with all your heart; don't let fear keep us apart. Long have I waited for your coming home to me and living deeply our new life." (The teenagers will remember it long after *A Hard Day's Night* has disappeared.) The associate pastor was there and called the experience awesome: God filled the church. Preaching Christ crucified without any histrionics or theatrics calls the Spirit to life. I share this experience not to give a kudo to Brennan but to testify to the power of the Word of God.

Father John Powell, S. J., spoke for three consecutive nights on prime-time television in Philadelphia during Holy Week of 1978 on man's image of God. When I returned there at Easter, the town — barbers, bartenders, policemen, housewives — was talking about nothing else. The life of the church will be revolutionized when the capital of our talents, personnel, and resources is invested in the ministry of evangelization.

When Emile Cardinal Leger left Montreal in 1969 to live in a leper colony in Africa, he said, "The time for talking is over." In the context of his own personal life, this was moving and valid. In the context of evangelization, the time for talking is just beginning.

> So I say to you: Ask and it will be given to you; search and you will find; knock and the door will be opened to you. For the one who asks always receives; the one who searches always finds; the one who knocks will always have the door opened to him. (Matthew 7:7-8; Luke 11:9-10)

Lord, I'm ducking again.
I've got a decision to make
that I've resolutely ignored
for some time now.
I'm behaving like the proverbial
ostrich;
ignore it long enough
and maybe it'll go away.
But things don't work that way
and I know it.
Some time I'm going to have to do
something
one way or the other.
And because this is important to me
I'm scared.
I don't want to decide;
I want to duck until it's too late
for me to decide anything.
I want somebody else
to make the decision for me;
somebody else to assume
the responsibility.
Then, if it's wrong,
I won't have to blame myself.

Lord, forgive me.

I seem to have forgotten
that if I ask

you'll tell me what to do.
You'll help me to decide
which way to go;
and if I ask,
you'll give me the courage
to follow your advice.

Lord, let me seek your will in this,
not mine.
And, having found it,
let your will become my own.

CHAPTER 15

ONE FOR THE ROAD

*T*he Hazelden Clinic in Minnesota for the rehabilitation of chemically dependent people is reputed to be the finest in the world. Thousands of alcoholics and drug abusers have been guided to inner peace and serene sobriety through its thirty-day program. One feature of the program is a series of low-key, tightly directed films on the debilitating effects of ingesting large quantities of booze.

It was a rainy Wednesday morning. About 150 residents were gathered in the auditorium. The film dealt with a lawyer in Canada who nipped at his office in the morning (the bottle was hidden behind a bookshelf of legal tomes), had a couple of martinis at lunch, stopped in at the neighborhood watering hole on his way home, and had several drinks with dinner. The blackouts began; the morning eye-opener became a necessity to stop the trembling. He had passed from heavy drinking to chronic alcoholism. A good-natured drunk who never got hostile or violent, he prided himself on his gentlemanly deportment.

One night while his distraught wife was doing the dishes, he mused how fortunate he was to have three such wonderful children. His favorite was the four-year-old, Meggie. First, he would have one for the road. Then he scooped her off the floor, carried her out to the car, and proudly announced, "Daddy and little Meggie-Weggie are going for a drive all by ourselves." He rolled down the driveway, made a right, and failed to see the red light. The film ended in the most grotesque auto accident I have ever seen, with

Meggie's dismembered body strewn all over the street.

The man sitting next to me in the auditorium bolted out of his seat, screaming, "For Christ's sake, stop it!" He ran out of the theater trying to bury his head in his hands. He had done the same thing to his three-year-old son.

In 2007, 41,059 Americans were killed in traffic accidents. Traffic authorities do not indulge in gratuitous guesswork. They categorically state that one-half of all auto accidents in the United States are alcohol related. Driving that endangers human life or property is immoral. Traffic safety, certainly, is more than a moral problem. For all the Meggies and their families in this country, it is an unspeakable tragedy.

Irresponsible driving, frequently combined with high speed and drunkenness, is a personal moral evil, even when an accident does not occur. Such a sin is more serious than many other moral transgressions we confess. It is a failure in full moral responsibility toward our neighbor.

Admittedly, there is nothing more obnoxious than a reformed drunk. But I do not write these words to preach at anybody or to lay the groundwork for another temperance union. This souvenir was written during one of the bleakest moments of my life, out of the anguish of my past and with trembling before what might have been. I've never had an accident or received a DUI (for driving under the influence), but I kneel before the Father of Mercies, asking forgiveness for my recklessness, my callous disregard for life, and I intercede for all the Meggies in this country, their families, and the poor wretches who still scream out in the night, "For Christ's sake, stop it!"

Lord, there's something
I have to discuss with you.
Just lately
some people I know
have been telling me
how good I am.
They've been telling me
I'm holy.
They'd make me out
to be a saint.
They credit me
with all kinds of virtues
I just don't have.
And while this may be great
for my ego,
it's not good
for my soul.
It bothers me, Lord.
My protestations
are considered modesty.
My denials
are considered humility.

Lord, let me keep
my footing.
Don't let me
climb up
on that pedestal.

Lord, you know what I am.
Don't let me forget that.

CHAPTER 16

FASTING AND PRAYER

"*J*ohn's disciples came to him with the objection, 'Why is it that while we and the Pharisees fast, your disciples do not?' Jesus said to them, 'How can wedding guests go in mourning so long as the groom is with them? When the day comes that the groom is taken away, then they will fast'" (Matthew 9:14-15).

The Italian psychologist Psichiari once remarked that "the best preparation for prayer is a handful of dates and a glass of water." Physical fasting from food is the joining of the body to the spirit's hunger for God. Even after a one-day fast, I find that I more readily enter the ardent longing for God expressed in Psalm 63: "O God, you are my own God whom I seek; for you my flesh pines and my soul thirsts like the earth, parched, lifeless and without water."

Fasting is the cry of the whole body-person, a yearning for the justice of God to be revealed. Therefore the Pharisees and John's disciples fasted. Jesus said, "You don't need to fast now. What you were hungry for, what you longed for, is here."

But why didn't they recognize Him? Well-intentioned men, assiduous in prayer and personal discipline, they missed the hour of visitation; they did not recognize Him as the fulfillment of the fullness of time. Why? The Jesuit priest Father Frank Miles, a veteran spiritual director, noted that in all his years of guiding people to the Lord, the greatest obstacle in the life of prayer and the greatest difficulty to union with God is *expectations*. Lord, I have fasted, denied myself, lost three pounds, and gone through the hammers of hell. Now I expect You to come in sweetness and joy, fill my heart with peace, and abundantly compensate for all that arduous fasting. Is this the criterion of good prayer? If so, the prayer of Jesus in the Garden of Gethsemane was a bummer.

I don't expect and I don't like a God who comes in failure, in loneliness, in poverty. Yet God comes to me where I live and loves me where I am. If I am not where I am, God cannot meet me. It's as simple as that. But when I remain where I am with everything that is moving inside me, salvation comes. Isn't that true in your own experience? The Lord is saying, "I don't want your profound thoughts, the magnanimous acts of love that slide so easily off your tongue, your burnt offerings and holocausts; I want your heart."

Late one night as I was driving to the Cenacle retreat house in New Orleans, I got drowsy at the wheel. I had just finished a charismatic workshop and had been fasting for three days. The fatigue overtook me, and I thought it prudent to stop at a motel. When I got to my room, I turned on the television to catch the news and sat down on the bed. I looked up at the screen and saw a wild sex orgy in progress. (I hadn't noticed the unilluminated sign "X-rated movies shown in room" when I entered.) I jumped to my feet and darted across the room to change the channel. Then I stopped in my tracks and returned to the bed. I lowered my head and prayed, "Lord, for three days I served Your people, fasted, and prayed. Honor my sincerity by not letting these impure images linger in my mind."

The images remained. "Deliver me from lust, Lord," I cried aloud. The inner turmoil continued. The liberating, redeeming Jesus of Nazareth was not living up to my expectations. Then came a word of truth: "Help yourself!"

Calmly, I said, "Lord Jesus, I really am getting sexually aroused and sense a growing excitement within me. But I prefer the pleasure of your friendship to the transitory turn-on of this erotica. I want You and nothing else." Then I got up and changed the channel.

What I learned from that experience was this: When I react in a panicky, irrational way to sexual stimuli, I succeed only in *repressing* the images into my subconscious; they come back to plague me later that night or the following day. When I cop a plea, "Deliver me, Lord," I exonerate myself from any further personal responsibility. But the poignant truth is, I have not made a *decision* for the lordship of Jesus Christ. Human beings are more godlike than any other species in the universe because we have the freedom to choose, to obey or refuse to obey. My spontaneous, programmed response was not only ungodlike and un-Christian, it was subhuman. I refused to deal with the temptation in a free and mature fashion. However, when I make a conscious personal *decision*, the sexual imagery is *suppressed* and will not return to haunt me later. In this context, temptation is less an enticement to evil than an invitation to love.

The Lord did not live up to my expectations. He came to me where I lived with all that was moving and stirring within me and empowered me to choose. And salvation came to my house.

Well, Lord, I fell off the diet again
with a resounding bang.
And I'm feeling guilty.
We both know
it's no longer a question
of simply losing weight.
We both know I'm sick.
I understand I have an illness
which can be controlled
only by a restricted diet.
And I should be
adult enough,

mature enough
to accept that fact
and stick with it.

But, Lord, you know how weak I am.
Especially when I'm hungry!
And last night I was so hungry
for all those things
I'm not allowed.
Lord, help me.
I can't do it on my own.

When I get hungry
remind me
of the hundreds of thousands
of your children
who are starving.
When I am tempted
and resent the limitations
of my diet,
remind me
of all those people
who would feel themselves
blessed
to have the amount of food
that diet allows me.

And, Lord, when I'm so hungry
I think I can't stand it,
feed me yourself
and I shall be satisfied.

CHAPTER 17

PENANCE

"Repent and reform your lives!" (Mark 1:15).
During my decades with the Franciscan community, I have engaged in some truly bizarre penitential practices, and I've seen others indulge themselves in a similar way. I cannot imagine any human relationship enduring, never mind improving, by these legalistic shenanigans.

Picture a husband and wife married two years with a little baby. It's five on Friday night, and the husband leaves his office. He longs to be with his wife and spend the night alone with her. Earlier he had called her during his lunch break. On the way home he picks up one long-stemmed red rose. He envisions his wife on the doorstep lighting up with joy at his arrival. She isn't there.

He enters the family room. She isn't there. He finds her at the dining room table writing. "Hi," he says. No reply. She hands him the list she has just completed. It's titled "The Things I've Done Today That Will Offend You": (1) spilt a drop of milk (value about four cents); (2) ironed your shirts carelessly; (3) twice while preparing dinner, I allowed my mind to wander from the thought of you.

"What the heck is going on?"

Solemn-faced, she hands him a second list: "The Things I've Done Today to Please You": (1) refused to turn on the television; (2) allowed the baby to cry without stopping all day; (3) ate a cheap, nauseating lunch just for you.

"Marie, are you all right?"

With hanging head and downcast eyes, she hands him the last list: "All the Things I Want You to Give Me."

He slumps into a chair in the family room. She turns the television on and sits at a distance. She stares at it. He realizes that they are miles and miles apart. They are both alone.

Perhaps the Lord smiles at the wacky ways we try to please Him. But the truth remains: We have not grasped the fundamental meaning of the Incarnation—that in becoming man, the Bridegroom is fully human, that He has a sensitive human heart and longs to be treated in a human way.

Evangelical penance has a twofold purpose: to overcome the disorder and disharmony in our lives and to deepen our relationship with Jesus Christ. It should be both corrective and productive. A dialogue at Wernersville, Pennsylvania, with Father George Schemel, S. J., on the subject "What is a suitable way to do penance?" was enlightening. A suitable approach to penance depends on how the spirit has been wounded. How have I grieved the spirit within me? How have I wounded myself? How have I burdened or damaged the vital, animating force in my life? Obviously, the most suitable way to do penance is to do that which revivifies and vitalizes the spirit within me. Rather like letting the punishment fit the crime.

For instance, if my desolation comes from all work and no play, then the suitable way to do penance may be to go to a symphony, a movie, or a ball game. It may be to take time off to visit my friends. If my desolation comes from undue loneliness, the suitable penance may be to make a serious effort to communicate my true thoughts to another or a group. If my desolation comes from feelings of insincerity and untruth, then a meaningful penance would be to open myself in sincerity and truth with my spiritual director. If my desolation comes from seeing that I'm getting nothing done through laziness, then a suitable penance would be some discipline that forces me to do some particular thing, such as write a letter, clean the oven, mow the lawn. The real question is, "How has the spirit been deadened?" The suitable penance must always be tailored to revivifying and reanimating the spirit.

It should be kept in mind that we are using *spirit* here in the scriptural sense. Spirit does not mean immaterial. We are talking about the person here. A person is a spirit-in-a-body-in-the-world. Spirit is not esoteric or disembodied. Matter and spirit are one. This was Paul's usage in his letters. When he said the spirit wars against the flesh, he was not thinking of some pneumatic being warring against our bones and flesh and blood (see Ephesians 6:12). The spirit for Paul *was* those bones and flesh and blood. The "flesh" for Paul was that person who has not under the aegis of faith. So spirit and matter are one.

When we speak, then, of the wounding of the spirit, we are not talking of some puff of gray steam that lives somewhere inside our heads or hearts. Nor are we speaking of the Holy Spirit, who dwells in our being. We are speaking of the wounding of the person — the total person. The person who sits here right now in sickness or in health, in joy or in sadness, in anger or in love, or whatever. This obviously brings the body much more into focus. It is scriptural, pre-Pauline, pre-Christ, and very contemporary.

Lord, sometimes I wish
you'd quit challenging me.
You're always at it.
Every time I turn around
you've got a new one
for me.
And your challenges
have a way
of turning everything
upside down.

They force me to change things
I'd like to leave alone.
They make me do things
I've never done before.
They knock all of the
complacency
out of me.
They're unsettling.

Forgive me, Lord,
for wishing you to stop
daring me
to learn,
to grow,
to give myself away,
to love,
to live.
Without those challenges
of yours
I'd die.

CHAPTER 18

THE CHILD AND THE PHARISEE

*G*rowth in the Spirit will eventually be a dead end if the Christian focuses only on the good guy/bad guy dichotomy in his personality, the opposition between the sinner and the saint. It gets to be unrealistic. His life has been purified of any serious moral flaws, and he is trying to be a loving man, yet he never arrives at the inner freedom God wants His children to have. At this juncture, it is helpful to focus on the child in me and the Pharisee in me.

The child represents my authentic self and the Pharisee the inauthentic. The aim of psychoanalysis is to move the client away from the falseness, the phoniness, the pseudosophistication in his life toward a childlike openness to reality, toward what Jesus enjoins us to be: "Unless you become as little children . . ." How long does a child bear a grudge, nurture bitterness, harbor resentment? One day out jogging I saw two boys about seven years old get into a fight. Being a true instrument of peace, I ducked into a doorway to watch the outcome. The heavier boy quickly got the mastery of the lighter, pinned his wrists to the ground, and asked, "Give up?" The vanquished surrendered. A minute later while dusting off their pants, the victor said, "Wanna piece of my bubble gum?" The other accepted, and they went off down the road arm in arm.

The Pharisees were virtuous but inauthentic. They did the

right things rightly, placated God (they felt), but were confined in a straitjacket of legalism, ritual, and externalities. They were closed to life, to grace, and to Jesus Christ. In some quarters today, the Pharisee could pass as "a good Christian." It is good to remember that the Gospels were written for all of us. They illustrate fundamental life situations; time and space are irrelevant. Mary Magdalen was sinful but open.

The child within is aware of all his feelings and moves freely in the Spirit to express them. The Pharisee within closes off feelings and makes a stereotyped response to life situations. The first time Jacqueline Kennedy was to visit the Vatican, Pope John XXIII asked his secretary of state, Cardinal Montini, what was the proper way to greet his visiting dignitary. The reply came, "It would be correct to say Madame or Mrs. Kennedy." The secretary left, and a few minutes later the president's wife stood in the doorway. The pope's eyes lit up; he trundled over, threw his arms around her, and cried "Jacqueline!"

The inner child is capable of a spontaneous breakthrough of emotions, but the Pharisee within represses them. This is not a question of being an emotional person or a subdued one. The issue is: Do I *express* or *repress* my authentic feelings? John Powell once said with sadness that if he had to write an epitaph for his parents' tombstone, it would say, "Here lie two people who never knew one another." His father could never share his feelings, so his mother never got to know him. To open yourself to another person, to stop lying about your loneliness, to stop lying about your fears and hurts, to be open about your affection, and to tell others how much they mean to you—this is the triumph of the child over the Pharisee and the dynamic presence of the Holy Spirit at work. "It was for liberty that Christ freed us" (Galatians 5:1).

I would like to suggest to you that there is a very special communication that is necessary in a love relationship. It is the communication of our feelings. You can share anything else with a person and not be close to the person. You can share food and money. You can even share sexual intimacy and not be too close to the other person. But there is one thing, I would suggest, that you cannot share with another person and not be close. The honest and open sharing of all feelings results in personal closeness and intimacy.

Your feelings reveal, as nothing else can, the real you. For example, I can stand up and say to you, "I am a priest." And you would reply, "Oh, come on, the woods are full of them." And I reply, "That's the essential commitment of my life." And you say, "Yeah, but you haven't told us very much about yourself. How does it feel to be a priest? Are you lonely? What is Saturday night like for you? When you walk down the street and there is a young loving couple walking in front of you holding hands, do you wish you had a hand you could hold? Do you sing in your heart 'Hello, Young Lovers, Whoever You Are'? How do you feel about these things?" If I tell you how I feel about these things, then you will get to know me. You can talk on the level of clichés or about other people and have all the news at your fingertips, or you can be the humorous person who keeps everyone laughing. But you don't really share yourself until you share your feelings. This, I think, is the secret of love.

Of course, it is risky to open up, to take in another person's feelings. It is difficult to listen sensitively and for a long time in order to say, "Yes, yes, I know what you are feeling." But that is what the inner child does and what the Pharisee flees.

The child is fresh; the Pharisee stale. The former is not necessarily peculiar or eccentric but simply does things in an original way. He may say the same things as other people do, but they are stamped with his own uniqueness and interiority. On Christmas Day in 1962, John XXIII visited Regina Coeli Prison on the shores of the Tiber. He was admitted to death row, and the prisoners were released from their cellblocks. He began to say a few encouraging words about the Child of Bethlehem, the great Light that has shone in our darkness, when the prisoners began to murmur, "The phony . . . comes down here on a token visit just to get his picture in the paper." The snickering continued. Pope John stopped speaking. So did the prisoners. "You are wondering why I came here this afternoon," he said. "I have come because I love you."

Certainly not an original expression, but it was fresh. The pontiff put himself on the line in risk and trust. The Pharisee would have had a preorganized, stale response because he could not open to suddenly unfolding life situations.

"Unless you become as little children . . ." The spiritual life might be defined as the development of personality in the realm of faith and grace. My Christian personality is not just a vegetative existence; I am a unique and radiant center of personal thought and feeling. Rather than living a routine existence in mere conformity with the crowd, the emerging child reminds me I have a face of my own, gives me the courage to be myself, protects me against being like everybody else, and calls forth that living, vibrant, magnificent image of Jesus Christ that is within me waiting only to unfold and be expressed.

Father, most of the time
I don't consider myself
much of a prize.
You know that
most of the time
I don't think of myself
as one of your
works of art.
But last night
you said to me,
"You are indeed
the work of my hands."

Artists don't always
sign their work,
I know;
sketches
and drafts
and those works
that don't please them,
if not destroyed,
are simply left
unsigned.

But you thought enough
of your work of art—
ME—
to emblazon me
with your signature.

Father, I may never think
of myself
as a masterpiece.
But thank you
for signing me
indelibly
and forever
with the gift
of your own Spirit.

CHAPTER 19

A DEBT OF GRATITUDE

Speculative theologians have fallen on hard times in recent days. Their focus of concern is widely regarded as a highly sophisticated, academic discipline, which is restricted to bespectacled scholars who reside in ivory towers, detached from the real world. Certain fundamentalists bemoan the futility of their efforts. "The speculative theologians," they say, "are so preoccupied with *heilsgeschicte* and *formgeschite*, hermeneutics and exegesis [I bowed my head when I heard the word], so busy spinning out someone's definition of nature, someone's idea of eschatology, someone's notion of religious pluralism, that there isn't any time for Jesus of Nazareth."

The pulse and heartbeat of my own interior life for many years has been a deepening relationship with the Father, the Abba of Jesus. My book *The Wisdom of Tenderness* was based on a deeply moving personal experience of His loving-kindness. Immediately upon awakening in the morning, my prayer begins, "Abba, I belong to You . . . Daddy, I belong to You . . ."(Seven syllables by the way. Inhale on "Abba," exhale on "I belong to you," and you will discover that this prayer corresponds perfectly to the natural rhythm of your breathing.) I have shared these insights with thousands of people all over this country and in Europe, and I have received countless letters of gratitude.

Thank you for introducing us to Abba, our Daddy!
Thank you for your obedience that has allowed the Holy

Spirit to speak this unforgettable message through you.
—Gene and Virginia Madian, San Jose, California

Your tape on "Abba" is all over the New York/New
Jersey area. You will never know the lives that have been
changed by this simple, powerful revelation.
—Helen Schneider, West Orange, New Jersey

I was so afraid of God, but now that I met my Daddy, I'm
not afraid anymore. —Pat De Rosa, Chicago, Illinois

So many lives have been touched, enriched, transformed
through the power of the Word of Jesus about His Father—and
my indebtedness to speculative theologians is inestimable. Their
insight, clarity, and emphasis on passages such as Mark 10:13-16,
Romans 8:14-17, and Galatians 4:4-7 brought the Word to life
in my heart. My own ministry has been largely a translation or
prayerful popularization of the seminal thinking of these Spirit-
filled men and women.

I wish to share four contributions relating to the Father that
have enhanced my own personal life and ministry:

Karl Rahner, in his book *Grace in Freedom*, said,

Even our most intimate, unique experiences happen in
our life because they encounter similar ones in other men,
and thus meet themselves. The history in which we live
our common life together is the place where everyone
finds himself. Now there we may find a man who called
himself simply the Son and who said "Father" when he
expressed the mystery of his life. He spoke of the Father
when he saw the lilies of the field in their beauty, or when
his heart overflowed in prayer, when he thought of the
hunger and need of men and longed for the consum-
mation that ends all the transitoriness of this seemingly

empty and guilty existence. With touching tenderness he called this dark, abysmal mystery, which he knew to be such, *Abba*, [i.e., "Father, dear Father"]. And he called it thus not only when beauty and hope helped him to overcome the incomprehensibility of existence in this world, but also when he met the darkness of death and the cup in which was distilled all the guilt, vanity and emptiness of this world was placed at his lips and he could only repeat the desperate words of the Psalmist: "My God, my God, why hast thou forsaken me!" But even then that other, all-embracing word was present to him, which sheltered even this forsakenness: "Father, into thy hands I commend my life."[1]

German Lutheran theologian Joachim Jeremias said,

We are now in a position to say why *abba* is not used in Jewish prayer as an address to God: to a Jewish mind, it would have been irreverent and therefore unthinkable to call God by this familiar word. It was something new, something unique and unheard of, that Jesus dared to take this step and to speak with God as a child speaks with his father, simply, intimately, securely. There is no doubt then that the *Abba* which Jesus uses to address God reveals the very basis of his communion with God. . . . Thus, when Jesus spoke of God as "my Father," he was referring not to a familiarity and intimacy with God available to anyone, but to a unique revelation which was bestowed upon him. He bases his authority on the fact that God has graciously endowed him with the full revelation, revealing himself to him as only a father can reveal himself to his son. *Abba*,

---

[1] Karl Rahner, *Grace in Freedom* (New York: Herder and Herder, 1969), 198.

then, is a word which conveys revelation. It represents the centre of Jesus' awareness of his mission.[2]

The next citation takes on a special vigor and pathos because it was written by Alfred Delp, a Jesuit priest facing the inevitability of death in a Nazi concentration camp.

> The word Father sounds strange in these surroundings. But it is constantly in my mind. Even in that ugly little room filled with hatred where men were making a travesty of justice, it never left me. In the past few months I have met nothing but hatred, enmity, pride and presumption from the people with whom I have been thrown into contact; nothing but ruthless force intoxicated with its own autocratic power and usurped dominion. It would be a terrible thing if the graceless life, to which today we are all subjected in one form or another, were the final revelation of reality. All we can do is to remember faithfully that God does call himself our Father, that we are bidden to call on him by that name and to know him as such—and that this pompous, self-important world in which we live is only the foreground to the center of reality which so many scarcely notice in the noise and tumult surrounding them. . . .
>
> God as Father, as source, as guide, as comforter; these are the inner resources with which a man can withstand the mass assault of the world. And this is no mere figure of speech—it is actual fact. The man of faith is aware of the solicitude, the compassion, the deepseated support of providence in innumerable silent ways even when he is attacked from all sides and the outlook seems hopeless.

---

[2] Joachim Jeremias, *The Central Message of the New Testament* (New York: Scribner, 1965), 21, 26–27.

God offers words full of wonderful comfort and encouragement; he has ways of dealing with the most desperate situations. All things have a purpose and they help again and again to bring us back to our Father.[3]

The last section is from the theologian/evangelist Robert Frost, who captured the warmth and tenderness of the Father's love in this beautiful commentary on Mark 10:13-16.

At this point the Scriptures say that some little children were brought to Him, probably by their parents. Possibly they were trying to gain entrance to the house, or as one commentator suggests, they may have been the children of the household who were introduced to Jesus . . . before going to bed. That indeed would be a tender touch to the story.

Obviously the parents sensed something of God's love in Jesus, and wanted their little children to be blessed and caressed by the Lord. They must have approached Jesus with a sense of warm expectation. I have tried to imagine the expression on the bright little faces of the children, as they looked up into the beautiful, loving eyes of Jesus. (I have always pictured Jesus with crinkle-marks by His eyes.) Such a lovely scene hardly prepares us for the rude response which follows.

The disciples, perhaps partly to protect their tired teacher, but maybe to relieve their own annoyance by such an interruption, sternly rebuke the parents and roughly push the children away from the Lord. There is a sudden change in attitude on the part of Jesus as with great indignation He turns to the disciples and sharply informs them that little children and the kingdom of God belong very much together.

---

[3] *The Prison Meditations of Father Alfred Delp* (New York: MacMillan, 1963), 105–106.

Once again His eyes soften and with outstretched arms He reassures the parents and calls the little ones unto himself. The Scriptures state that He took them in His arms one by one and placed His hands upon them, and fervently blessed them (Mark 10:16, TAB). I am so glad Jesus didn't suggest they group all the children together for sort of a general blessing because He was rather tired. Instead, He took time to hold each child close to His heart and to earnestly pray for them all . . . they then joyfully scampered off to bed.

One is tenderly reminded of a beautiful messianic passage from the prophets:

> He will feed His flock like a shepherd,
> He will gather the lambs in His arm,
> He will carry them in His bosom, and
> will gently lead those that have their
> young. (Isaiah 40:11, TAB)

Besides the deeper truths concerning the character of the kingdom, what else is Jesus trying to convey through this vivid account recorded in all three of the synoptic Gospels? Isn't this a perfect picture of the lovingkindness of our heavenly Father? It is as if Jesus is saying, "Look, this is the way your Father-God feels about you. He wants to hug you to His heart, and personally bless your life with His love and mercy." I think there is also a lesson here for any who would seek to set any kind of false condition concerning just who should be recipients of God's grace. He blessed them all![4]

---

[4] Robert Frost, *Our Heavenly Father* (Plainfield, NJ: Logos International, 1978), 43–44.

God forbid the day should ever come when the people of God disdain the discipline of the speculative theologians and demand that they come down from their ivory towers to where it's really at! That will be the dark day when we head for the shallows to avoid the deeps.

Father, you must have known
I was feeling like the day:
dull
grey
dismal
with a tendency
to thunderstorms.

And so you flung
a rainbow
across the sky
and whispered
coaxingly
in my ear,
"Look at what
I've made—
just for you."

And as I looked
wondered
marveled
what really
took my breath away
wasn't the splendor
of your creation,

but the breathtaking
mind-boggling
heart-stopping
realization
that I am a pampered
petted
cherished
child.
Indulged.
Highly favored.
Given all.

Father, thank you
for the love
that made the rainbow
just for me.

And, Father, make me like
your rainbow.
Let me
reflect
the spectrum
of your love.

CHAPTER 20

CREATION

Why did God make the world? Theology says, *"Bonum diffusum sui"* — "good diffuses itself." However, the meaning of this lapidary little phrase may not be apparent immediately. Theology says that God is one in essence and triple in personality. Theology speaks of the divine monarchy of the Father as the fount and origin of all being. Theology speaks of the doctrine of *perichoresis* (Greek) or *circumincession* (Latin), the coinherence whereby the three divine Persons mutually indwell one another because they are one God. Creation is the overflow of the eternal generation of God's infinite love. This being said, we return to the original question: Why did God make the world?

The whole sense of Scripture, it seems to me, is that God the Father had this thing about being. He was absolutely wild about it. He kept thinking up new ways of being and new kinds of being to be. One afternoon God the Son came along and said, "This is really great stuff; why don't I go out and mix Us up a batch?" And God the Holy Spirit said, "Terrific! I'll help You."

So they got together that night after supper and put on a tremendous show of being for the Father. It was full of water and light and frogs; pussy willows kept dropping all over the place, and crazy fish swam around in the wine glasses. There were mushrooms and grapes, horseradishes and tigers; and men and women everywhere to taste them, to juggle them, to join with them and love them. God the Father looked at the whole wild party and said, "Wonderful! Just what I had in mind. Yay, yay, yay!" And all God the Son and God the Holy Spirit could think of to say was, "Yay, yay, yay!" They laughed for ages and ages, saying things like how great it was for being to be, how clever of the Father to conceive the idea, how kind of the Son to go to all the trouble of putting it together, and how considerate of the Spirit to spend so much time directing and choreographing. Forever and ever they told old jokes to one another all over again, and the Father and the Son drank their wine in the unity of the Holy Spirit, and they threw ripe olives and pickled mushrooms at each other *per omnia saecula saeculorum* (forever and ever).

Admittedly, it is a crass analogy. But I'm growing convinced that crass analogies are the safest. Everyone knows that God is not really a bearded old man throwing olives. Not everyone, I'm afraid, is equally convinced that God is not a cosmic force, a mere uncaused Cause or immovable Mover, or anything else we might choose to call Him. Accordingly, I present the image (much closer to the truth than these others) that creation is the result of a hilarious, Trinitarian bash and leave you to sort out the minor details for yourself.

Creation, Scripture says, is good. Created things are just so many myriad responses to the delight of God who wills them into being. St. Thomas Aquinas would say, *"Ens in quantum ens es bonum. Ens et bonum convertuntur."* ("Being is good in itself. Being and good are interchangeable.")

Admittedly, it is not always easy to see that all being is good. Earthquakes and poison toadstools, cancer cells, liver flukes, killer whales, and loan sharks have to be considered. But there is no going back on what the book of Genesis records: "God looked at everything he had made, *and he found it very good.*" (Genesis 1:31, emphasis added). Creation is a response to the vast delight of God. Man is basically good. His human nature, fallen but redeemed, is freed from the slavery of sin and capable of the heights of holiness. The body, risen with Christ in baptism, is a sacred vessel, a shrine of the imperishable Spirit. (We could do with a good deal less of the pessimism about man found in certain Christian circles.)

Robert Frost said,

> The Lord once brought me up short with the challenge: "Why do you persist in seeing your children in the hands of the devil, rather than in the hands of their faithful Shepherd?" I then realized that in my mind I had been imagining all of the evils of our present age as being ultimately more powerful than the timeless love of God.[1]

Pain, inconvenience, sin — these are the *problems* of being, the alarming, embarrassing, even tragic things that God is apparently willing to put up with in order to have beings at all. But whatever the problems are, they are not the *root* of being. That root is *joy* and now.

It is important to recapture the *element of delight* in creation. Imagine the ecstasy, the veritable orgy of joy, wonder, and delight when God makes a person in His own image — when God made you. The Father gave you as a gift to Himself. You are a response to the vast delight of God. Out of an infinite number of possibilities, God invested you with existence. Regardless of the mess you may have made out of the original clay, wouldn't you agree with Aquinas that "it is better to be than not to be"?

Have I really appreciated the wonderful gift that I am? Could the Father's gift to Himself be anything but beautiful? I love His other gifts: His pussy willows and pussycats, rainbows and rivers and sunsets. I'd ride more merry-go-rounds and pick more daisies. I'd eat a lot more ice cream and less beans. I'd go barefoot earlier in the spring and stay out later in the fall. I'd climb more mountains and swim more lakes. I'd take more trips, but most of all I would love Jesus Christ and those around me, and I would let them know before life's evening.

---

[1] Robert Frost, *Our Heavenly Father* (Plainfield, NJ: Logos International, 1978), 130.

Perhaps the main reason that we are such poor practitioners of the art of being human, why we so often teeter on a tightrope between self-hatred and despair, is that we don't pray. We pray so little, so rarely, and so poorly. For everything else we have adequate leisure time. Visits, get-togethers, movies, football games, concerts, an evening with friends, an invitation we can't decline—and these are good because it is natural and wholesome that we come together in community. But when God lays claim on our time, we balk. Do we really believe that He delights to talk with His children? If God had a face, what kind of face would He make at you right now?

Would His face say, "When are you going to shape up? I'm fed up with you and your hang-ups. My patience is exhausted. We're going to have a little reckoning"? If God said only one word to you, would the word be "repent"? Or would He say, "Thank you. Do you know what a joy it is to live in your heart? Do you know that I have looked upon you and loved you from all eternity?" What would God say? What is the feedback you get from your Creator?

If it is discouraging feedback, nonaffirming feedback, then quite naturally you will find a thousand brilliant excuses for not praying. If the God who sees right through you is always reminding you of your weakness and infidelity, you will find very little joy in your acts of religion and worship. With this kind of nagging feedback, you become a shriveled old fig. Even if you hang in there, being religious, when they bury you, you will look like a fig. You may have kept all your virtue intact and never missed church on Sunday, but oh, it was awful. What a bummer! You never lived; you never opened yourself to God. You never said, "Oh, Abba, Daddy, You do love me, don't You?"

If you believe that you are a response to the vast delight of God in His creation and that He delights to talk with His children, you will hear Him answer, "Yes, I have always loved you."

According to my little pal Sister Robin Stratton, a discalced

Carmelite tucked away in the Baltimore, Maryland, Carmel, this
is precisely what creation has to teach us:

Somebody once said, sang, or lived:
"You're nobody 'til somebody loves you."
It's true.

We remain a nonentity, no being,
nothing
timeless
spaceless
emotionless
complete ineffectiveness
until loved.

Then somebody comes along
and the world begins.
I begin.

For I realize that I'm not just a figment of my own
        imagination.
Only when I see the glow in another's eyes
do I know that I'm on fire.
Only when I see the explosion in another's life
do I see my own power.

Then and only then can I say,
"How about that! How about me!"

So often we spin our virtues, qualities, talents,
We spin our *usness* about us
Around and around we go
Peeping out now and then

Kind of confused and afraid
because we're not sure of what we're doing.
We can't see any reflection of *usness*
in somebody else.

Then the shell is cracked,
and somebody peeks in and says,
"Hi."
And then it's all real
because somebody else has it.

Suddenly *usness* exists outside the shell
outside us.
There it is:
We can see it,
feel its power,
watch its influence.
And it's great
looking at us from the outside.

What do you do?
Do you laugh
or cry
or sing
or shake hands with you?

Do you hug this blessed event
or just walk around
shaking your head?

You do all this and much more
until the thought hits you —
That's why Jesus is my brother and Lord!
Because He loves me.

A just here me
A just physical-matter me
or even an animated-matter me
is a not-much me.

But when He peeks in and says,
"Hi"
When He takes this "*usness*"
examines it, really looks it over, and says,
"I love you"
Then I have real-life existing me.
Then I have time
Then I have space
Then I'm alive (if you want — kicking).

That's why God said,
"You will be My people,
My bride,
My vineyard,
the apple of My eye."

When He loved us,
we began to exist as new creations
as persons, not as things.

The Gospel says:
"You are to be like
your brother Jesus."
Well then,

GO LOVE SOMEONE
GO CREATE SOMEONE
GO MAKE SOMEONE COME ALIVE
LET THEM SEE THEIR *USNESS* IN YOU!

"By this shall all men know
that you are my disciples
if you love . . .
The two greatest are
Love God
Love your neighbor."

And what if the opposite is true?
What if I give God existence
to the extent that
I love Him?

And really somehow
He doesn't have time
He doesn't have space
He doesn't have influence
He doesn't have emotion
Unless and until
And to the extent
I love Him.

Maybe I can't
put words to this
But deep down where it counts
I know it.

I know when He exists
and when He's the figment of my imagination.
It's when I refuse to let Him love me.
In the isolation of
and the egocentricity of
sin and the sinful situation
I know He is dead.
There's no life here
neither human nor divine.

Is this why (the real reason)
He was crucified?
Wasn't He dead long before Calvary?
When men refused to love Him—
refused to accept His kind of creation?

And really now— in the loveless situation
in the closed situation
in the hate situation
Can't you see *SMALL CALVARY*?[2]

Father, you have
so many
wonderful friends.
Thank you
for sharing them
with me.
Thank you
for sending me
people
to love;
people
who love me.

Thank you
for sharing them
with me,
these friends of yours,
who have done so much
and make me happy.

---

[2] Sister Robin Stratton, O. C. D., "Creation."

*Thank you, Father, for Jesus
and the gift of his friendship.*

CHAPTER 21

THE EASTER MAN

*M*odern theology's preoccupation with the resurrection of Jesus Christ is not apologetic. His Easter triumph is no longer simply viewed as proof par excellence that establishes the truth of Christianity. All New Testament scholars agree that the Resurrection actually occurred and the force of the gospel flows from it. For example, the teaching of the Sermon on the Mount is powerful because the risen Jesus stands by it and thereby gives it its final and present meaning.

If Jesus did not rise, we can safely praise the Sermon on the Mount as a magnificent ethic. If He did, praise does not matter. The sermon becomes a portrait of our ultimate destiny. Faith means that those who believe in the Resurrection receive the gospel message, and it reshapes them in the image and likeness of God. The meaning of the Resurrection is inseparable from the teaching of Jesus. The gospel reshapes the hearer through the power of the Resurrection. The gospel claims there is a hidden power in the world: the living presence of the risen Christ. It liberates man from the slavery that obscures the image and likeness of God in men.

The living presence of Jesus is His resurrection, and I should be experiencing its power. As Paul wrote to the Philippians, "I wish to know Christ and the power flowing from His resurrection" (3:10). In some way, Jesus rises in the faith of the community, and the Resurrection is present to us. Clearly then, Easter is not just another day in the weary round of time. It is the day of days, the feast of feasts, the center of the gospel and our whole Christian religion. Every time we celebrate Eucharist, we renew the *pesach* of Jesus—His breakthrough from death to life. Around the table that ancient Hebrew cry of joy and wonder becomes our own: "Alleluia, Alleluia, Alleluia! Christ is risen; death could not hold Him. Now He lives no more to die." In the words of St. Augustine, "We are Easter men, and Alleluia is our song."

The Easter man and woman know that Jesus was not obsessed with the thought of death but voluntarily submitted to it so that He might become, in the bold words of Paul, "the Son of God in power" (Romans 1:4). The Easter man and woman know that through their own water baptism they were caught up in the triumph of Jesus over death, that there they received the seed of eternal life, and that one day that seed will burst into glory.

The Easter man and woman are *realists*. They know that no human happiness can ever be complete because eventually death will end it. They know that death may come when they're old and feeble or when they're young, in the prime of life, filled with vigor and plans for the future. Death may come with a cancer microbe, a speeding car, a cloud of radioactive fallout. It came to six million Jews in the extermination camps in Nazi Germany; it came to 140,000 Japanese in the rubble of Hiroshima; it comes to tens of thousands each year on our highways. The Easter man and woman know that eventually it will come to them and that they must die their own death.

But if they are realists, they are also *optimists*. Like Hemingway's hero in *Death in the Afternoon*, they go forward to meet death courageously for death is no longer a fearful thing. Jesus Christ, their risen Savior, has conquered death. Its power has been snapped forever. In the words of St. Athanasius, the Easter man knows "that in dying he no longer perishes; that the Resurrection will render him incorruptible." Whatever the resurrected Christ has passes to the Christian by virtue of our baptismal union with Him. The grief of human separation notwithstanding, dying does not depress the Easter man. Death is essentially a joyous affair for it does not mark the end of anything; rather, it marks the beginning, the triumphant new beginning of a glorified life with Jesus Christ, who is but the firstborn of many brothers (see Romans 8:29) to penetrate the inner apartments of eternity. The spirit of the Easter woman is beautifully captured in the German Lutheran martyr Dietrich Bonhoeffer. On April 9, 1945, as he was being led to the gallows in a concentration camp in Flossenbürg, Germany (Bonhoeffer had conspired in a plot to assassinate Adolf Hitler), he broke loose from the two SS guards and went running toward the noose shouting, "O Death, you are the supreme festival on the road to Christian freedom."

The Easter man and woman have their eyes fixed on Jesus, "the author and pioneer of faith" (Hebrews 12:2), who claimed that death was finished, that He had the answer to the problem of death; to prove it, He would rise from the dead. "Destroy this temple," Jesus told the Pharisees, "and in three days I will raise it up." They retorted, "This temple took forty-six years to build, and you are going to raise it up in three days!" Actually, He was talking about the temple of His body (see John 2:19-21). Clearly, the Pharisees thought Jesus was out of His mind, but He was gathering a large following. So they put Him to death and sealed His tomb with a stone—only the tomb wouldn't stay closed, and the man came back to haunt His murderers and every man who has ever lived after Him. The Easter man knows that it is more than remotely possible that He was right, that He did have the answer to the problem of death, that His followers could cry out securely, invincibly, triumphantly, "O death, where is your victory; death, where is your sting?" Death, you are a phantom, the bogeyman of little children! The only reason my Father allows you to exist is to usher me into the one experience deserving of the name Life.

Since the question has been raised, and since the hope it has generated has been kept alive for two millennia, there are no other logical alternatives than these: You believe in the Resurrection and hence you believe in Jesus of Nazareth, or you believe in non-Resurrection and you do not believe in Jesus of Nazareth. If Easter is not history, we must become cynics. Either we believe in the Resurrection and a living Jesus who is with us in faith and we commit our whole lives to Him, or we do not. Either we dismiss the Good News as too good to be true, or we permit ourselves to be overwhelmed by the joyfulness of it and become overwhelmingly joyful persons because of it. The Christian is called to believe in a God who loves and His Christ who is risen. She believes, and she believes strongly; she believes, and she believes joyously. As theologian Robert Hotchkins once wrote,

> Christians ought to be celebrating constantly. Their lives ought to be occupied by parties, feasts, banquets and merriment, and they ought to give themselves over to veritable orgies of joy because of their belief in the Resurrection promise. They ought to attract people to their faith quite literally by the fun there is in being a Christian.

French writer Hilaire Belloc's oft-quoted rhyme captures the Christian vision:

> Wherever a Christian sun doth shine,
> There's always laughter and good red wine.
> At least I've always found it so,
> Benedicamus Domino!

Realist and optimist, the Easter woman is also an *idealist*. She knows that she must walk worthy of her high vocation as a member of the Easter People of God. Each Christian Sabbath as she enters the temple of the Lord and makes the sign of the cross with baptismal water, she reminds herself of her primary identity—daughter of the Father in Christ Jesus through the gift of the Holy Spirit. She vows anew to die to sin, selfishness, dishonesty, and any form of degraded love. "But the foundation God has laid stands firm. It bears this inscription: 'The Lord knows those who are his'; and 'Let everyone who professes the name of the Lord abandon evil'" (2 Timothy 2:19).

Finally, the Easter man is a *liturgist*. In faith he knows that he encounters the risen Christ in the Eucharist just as personally as Mary Magdalen met Him in the garden, just as really as Paul encountered Him on the road to Damascus. The Easter man knows that the Eucharist is mystery—not simply the celebration of a historically past event, such as the Fourth of July celebrating American freedom on Bunker Hill or a Thanksgiving Day celebration recalling the landing of the Pilgrim fathers on Plymouth Rock. In what Thomas Aquinas called "the supreme demonstration of God's love for His people," Jesus renews, reactualizes, re-presents His *pesach*—the mystery of His death and resurrection. It all really happens under the veil of sign and symbol, and the Christian community is swept up once more into the greatest act of love the world has ever known. Once again, in the words of Augustine, "We are Easter men, and Alleluia is our song."

The great Russian writer Nicholas Arseniew, in his book *Mysticism and the Eastern Church*, told the story of Comrade Lunatscharsky. He was lecturing in Moscow's largest assembly hall shortly after the Bolshevik Revolution. His theme: "Religion: Opium of the People." He said, "All the Christian mysteries are fabricated legends; Marxist science is the light that more than substitutes for the fables of Christianity." He spoke at great length. When he finished, he was so pleased with himself that he asked, in an expansive gesture, whether anyone in the audience wanted to ask a question or say anything.

A young Russian Orthodox priest stepped forward. First, he apologized for his ignorance and awkwardness. The commissar looked at him scornfully. "I'll give you five minutes, no more!" he snorted.

"I won't take very long," the priest replied.

He mounted the platform, turned to the audience, and in a loud voice declared, "Christ is risen!" With one voice the vast audience roared in response, "He is truly risen."

May that response find an echo in your heart and mind today. For the resurrection of Jesus Christ from the dead is the source, the reason, the basis for the inarticulate joy of our Christian lives. Christ is risen, Alleluia! One day His glory will shine forth in us. In the words of Augustine, we are Easter men and women en route to the heavenly Jerusalem; and on the journey, Alleluia is our song.

Lord, it's a glory hallelujah day.
The morning is as bright
as a new penny;
as fresh and as sweet
as a daffodil.
Somewhere a mocking bird
in the willows
behind the levee
is thanking you
for the gorgeous day
you've given us.

Let me join my voice
to his hymn of praise, Lord,
and thank you
for this shining Easter morn
when all your world
looks new.

Epilogue

*T*his little odyssey, spanning ten years of my life, is over, and I pray it has disturbed you as it disturbs me. That would be good, for as Pope John XXIII once said, "To be at ease is to be unsafe." Disturbance leads to conversion, and conversion leads to the Lord.

The Word has never received a rousing reception. In fact, they said, "He is out of his mind" (Mark 3:21, NIV). The teaching of Jesus as a set of propositions is foolish to the philosophers of this world. As a lifestyle, it is madness—losing your life to find it, renouncing self, hopping around like a sparrow unperturbed about tomorrow. When the crowd first heard it, even His family said, "He is out of his mind."

Perhaps somewhere in these pages, the Lord asked something of you that's driving you out of your mind. Maybe He gently invited you to let go of some attachment so that you might have more of Him. Be at peace. Whatever it is, you can't will it, disavow it, or empty yourself of it. It is only the power of a Presence, the compelling attractiveness of a Person, the irresistible loveliness of Jesus Christ that can set you free. Bernard of Clairvaux wrote, "Only he who has experienced it can believe what the love of Jesus is."

The Lord comes to you where you live and loves you as you are. Prayer is the art of the possible. Begin with forty minutes a day of prime time praying over the Scriptures for an intimate, heartfelt knowledge of Jesus. You will notice something abuilding.

Fire! The Spirit setting your feet a-dancing, your mind a-churning, and your heart a-burning. Then brace yourself for the ultimate compliment: "You're out of your mind!"

I shall close by sharing one of those moments of fire that light up my life so infrequently. In my journal, I wrote,

The snow has added a beautiful dimension to this retreat. The white blanket creates a sense of oneness, as though the earth, trees, and sky had made a clandestine covenant of unity. The landscape is a vast, uncluttered wilderness steeped in silence. Blowing where it will, the wind whispers, "I have lured you here, led you out into this desert that I might speak tenderly to your heart."

The courthouse and schools are closed, public transportation is paralyzed, the roads are deserted and northeastern Pennsylvania is a whited world of inward stillness. No mail, no telephone, no sound but the wind whistling through the trees. Yahweh, the Lord of hosts who made the Pleiades and the Orion, speaks: "I have muted the music of nature. I have said to the sky, 'Be silent,' and told the earth, 'Be still,' for I would speak to My beloved. Look out the window, little one. Nature lies dying. Do you heard My word, 'I'm dying to be with you'? Come away with Me. I don't want your prose, your penances, your prayers. I have come for your heart. Sshh! Be still and know that you are Mine and I am yours. No one will tear you from My hand. I want your prose to become poetry, your speech to become song, your myopia to become clear vision: *You are Mine; you belong to Me. I am yours. I am your God. Rejoice in the promise that is yours. Rejoice in hope of THE GLORY TO WHICH YOU ARE CALLED.*'"

Make ready for my Christ,
whose smile,
like lightning,
sets free the song of everlasting glory
that now sleeps in your paper flesh like dynamite.

—Thomas Merton

AN EIGHT-DAY
RETREAT FOR THE
READER

*T*his exercise will not require flight to the desert, a cave, or a retreat house. Its only exigency is to snatch, cost what it may, forty minutes of prime time each day for a prayerful pondering of the Word of God. "Prime time" refers to that hour when you are at your best — most alive and alert. However inconvenient, the early-morning hours are most highly recommended. George Maloney, S. J., wrote in *Inscape,*

> There can be little progress in deep faith, hope and love if one does not carve out the first moments of consciousness as the first fruits of the day and consecrate them to God in deep silence and adoration. . . .
>
> The success of our day will depend on our *centering* deeply in the early moments of the day before we become too "distracted" by the multiple activities that fill our busy lives. If we put such *centering* off until the afternoon or evening, we can see that we will meet the daily events only with our own power. We will judge according to St. Paul's "carnal mind." . . .
>
> And yet how few Christians are ready to give God daily the first hour of consciousness in which they can

humbly beg His mercy and love and surrender themselves in loving service to Him?[1]

First Day—Psalm 103. This prayer opened the door to a beautiful faith-filled experience of the Father. Gentle waves of peace washed over me. The words "Bless the Lord, O my soul, and forget not all his benefits. He pardons all your iniquities, he heals all your ills. He redeems your life from destruction. He crowns you with kindness and compassion" caused a sense of deep gratitude for the many times He has rescued me. Later the words "Not according to our sins does he deal with us, nor does he require us according to our crimes" put me in touch with His presence, and I began to praise Him for His greatness and goodness, His unbearable forgiveness, His boundless patience, His tender love. I felt as if my heart were fused with the psalmist's. Now the psalm is *my* prayer. "For as the heavens are high above the earth, so surpassing is His kindness toward those who fear Him. . . . As a father has compassion on His children, so the Lord has compassion on those who fear Him."

Carl and Norma Prask of North Hollywood, Florida, sent me a sculpture. The artist had chiseled a father cradling his little son on his instep and rocking him back and forth. The child is looking at his father with utter confidence and love. But suppose the little one deliberately slipped off his father's instep and walked away. How would the father feel? How would you feel? Would you miss your little one? Would you call out his name? Would you be eager for his return? In the interim, would you love him in his absence? Well, the Abba of Jesus is at least as nice a person as you.

Lord, it's almost too good to be true.
But you are the truth

---

[1] George A. Maloney, *Inscape: God at the Heart of Matter* (Denville, NJ: Dimension Books, 1978), 165–167.

and you said it,
so I know it's real.

Today I asked you
to speak to my heart,
a word I could hear
and understand.

And you said, very clearly,
"I want you to be with me
where I am."

Lord, even the people
who love me most
need a vacation
from me
now and then.

But you don't want one!
You want me with you
where you are
forever!

Lord!
The feeling's mutual!

SECOND DAY—PSALM 105. The words brought a peaceful reassurance that if God remained faithful to Israel despite her repeated infidelities, if only she turned to Him, He will not abandon me. Overall, the movement of the psalm made me ever so conscious of how totally dependent I am on God. He brought me out of darkness into light, from the feeling of being Mr. Nobody to the experience of being a dearly loved child, just as I am. His gifts are the lifeblood of my existence. I pray for the gift of a deeper faith, to be seized and captured by the awareness that I belong totally to Him and am totally possessed by Him and am called to live totally for Him. I pray for the courage to pronounce the word God spoke when He called me into being—the word that is my real name in His eyes.

Lord, have I ever thanked you
for your north wind?
If I haven't,
I do so now.

You must've known I was saturated
with summer.
This morning I walked out
and your blithe north wind
bit my cheek
and tangled my hair
and sent me scurrying
to the warmth of the waiting car,
accompanied by the cats,
prancing and dancing down the walk,
as if heralds of your wind
from the north.

Lord, your north wind
delights me,
invigorates me,
renews me.
It invites me
to walk faster,
breathe more deeply,
look more closely.
It brings
a wine-red promise

of crisp cold nights
bright with stars,
frosted windows
and warm beds
heaped high
with fluffy blankets.

Lord, it even has a different smell,
as though along the way to me
it picked up bits and pieces
of spruce and fir and juniper
and tar and salty seas,
mountain lakes
and spices.

I know, Lord, that to some
your bright north wind
brings only the promise
of hard, deep cold
and pain.
And I ask you, Lord,
to warm them
and to comfort them.

But as for me, my Lord,
I give you praise
and thanks,
honor and glory and blessing
for the sheer joy and exuberance
of your playful north wind
this morning.

THIRD DAY—JOHN 3:22-36. John the Baptist knew who he was and what he was called to be. "I am not the Messiah; I am sent before Him. It is the groom who has the bride. The groom's best man waits there, listening for him, and is overjoyed to hear his voice. That is my joy, and it is complete. He must increase, while I must decrease."

Who am I? What are my reasons for wanting to go on living? What are my goals, dreams, desires, aspirations? What is stirring, moving, surfacing in my soul? In a broad stroke of the brush, I would say, paraphrasing Thoreau, that as the hour of my particular sunset approaches, I would be appalled to discover that I had died without having lived. With Graham Greene's whisky priest, I would be deeply grieved if, as I reviewed my life, I had to repeat, "Ah, with just a little more courage, I could have become a saint."

First, I want a more intimate relationship with Jesus. The taste for prayer has returned, and I want to cultivate it. That will demand discipline of my time—for example, getting to bed by eleven thirty. I want to cut in half the work that presently consumes me and do the remaining half with contemplative vision and creative love. I stake the authenticity of my life and ministry on this radical shift. I want to stop taking myself so seriously and anyone who takes himself or herself seriously. I want to preach the Good News and share with others the beautiful gift I have received. I want to rely more and more on the vast resources of His power and overcome the timidity in my life. I want to live a simpler, poorer life. I want to be remembered not as a preacher, teacher, priest, or writer but as a loving man who resembled Jesus and lived for the Father.

Lord, I don't know why
I'm so surprised
when you take me literally.
I said to you, so often,
"Use me, Lord.
Make me your instrument."

And you took me at my word,
and things began to happen.

I suddenly discovered
that it isn't always
easy
or pleasant
or even comfortable
to be used by you.
I began to find out things
about myself
that I didn't like.

I discovered that I didn't mind
being used by you
so long as I wasn't inconvenienced;
so long as I wasn't asked to give
what I wasn't willing to share;
so long as it didn't hurt too much.
I began to learn
that being an instrument
requires an awful lot of humility.

Forgive me, Lord,
for my lack of humility;
for my dearth of charity.
Continue to teach me
what it means to be used by you.
And, using me,
keep teaching me
to know myself.

FOURTH DAY—LUKE 12:22-32. Here Jesus is talking about dependence on providence. Hmmm! In his book *On Being a Christian*, Hans Kung referred to St. Francis as "the clown of the millennium." In 1924, G. K. Chesterton used a similar phrase of Francis—"Jongleur de Dieu"—the clown of God. In the circus a clown often stands on his head. The result, of course, is that he sees the world upside down. Now, although your images of New Orleans may be incongruously arrested by Hurricane Katrina photos, play with me a bit. Suppose you drove by the Superdome (now completely repaired) in New Orleans and took a long look at this huge, circular block of granite. It would appear secure, permanent, immovable. But suppose in your mind's eye you saw it upside down. It wouldn't differ in a single detail except in being entirely the other way around. But now the massive weight would make it seem helpless and in grave peril. You would see and admire the dome as much as ever, but now you would see it in the divine light of eternal danger and dependence. Instead of being proud to show off this New Orleans landmark to visiting relatives, you would be thankful to God that it had not been dropped. And if you saw the French Quarter, the Hilton, the Lake Pontchartrain Bridge, and the whole city in this topsy-turvy fashion, you would be grateful to God for not dropping New Orleans like a crystal chandelier to be shattered beyond repair. In Latin, the word *dependere* means "to hand from." How did Francis the clown catch the idea of the world's total dependence on the providence of God? I do not think I will ever understand the noble thing we call "praise" without a Franciscan vision of reality!

> *Lord, today I tried to run the world*
> *singlehandedly.*
> *I tried so hard, Lord,*
> *to take care of everything.*

I took upon myself
all of the problems,
all of the burdens,
all of the worries
of everyone
who makes up my little world.
I tried so hard, Lord,
and I accomplished nothing.
I'm frustrated,
frazzled,
and exhausted to the point of tears.
Nothing seemed to go right.

Lord, will I never learn
that you're the one
who runs everything?
That you're the one
who knows all the answers?
That you're the only one
who can carry
the intolerable burdens
we try to shoulder for ourselves?
That you're the only one
who can solve
the insoluble problems?
That you're the only one
who accomplishes
anything of worth?
That everything depends on you?

Lord, sometimes I wonder why
you bother to put up with me.
Sometimes I wonder
if you're not sorely tempted

to take me by the shoulders
and shake me 'til my teeth rattle.
I couldn't blame you if you did.

Thank you, Lord,
for putting up with me today.

And thank you, Lord,
for doing things
YOUR way!

FIFTH DAY—HEBREWS 10:5-7. "Sacrifice and offerings you did not desire, but a *body* you have prepared for me; holocausts and sin offerings you took no delight in. Then I said, 'As it is written of me in the book, I have come to do your will, O God'" (emphasis added). Psychologists tell us that a man understands himself in terms of his spontaneous body image; what he feels about his *body* and its worth is what he feels about himself. What is my feeling about my body? The question might seem vain, superficial, and pretentious until we ask, How did Jesus Christ understand His body? A body that was broken for us: a sacrificial self, effective only through its destruction.

What is a beautiful male body? A face like Brad Pitt and a physique like Arnold Schwarzenegger? What is a beautiful female body? Thirty-eight–twenty-two–twenty-six? With a face like Cindy Crawford? That's the world, man! That's the flesh! That's what television commercials are all about. Father Rod McKenzie, the Jesuit biblical scholar in Rome, said,

> If you want to see the optimal use of the seven capital sins, just take note of what Madison Avenue does with ads on television. They appeal to all the capital disorders in our being. This is the language of the world (1 John 4:1-6) which appeals to our desire to be beautiful and successful,

our desire to be loved and recognized, our fear of suffering. This is what St. John is talking about when he speaks of the "world." The spirit of the world (in the Johannine sense) is not a matter of vanity of appearance, dress, acquisitions, etc. The spirit of the world moves a person to seek physical beauty and success and avoid suffering.

Look at your body. Is it too fat or too skinny or just trim? Is it flabby or muscular? Are you pleased or displeased? What are your criteria for feeling good about your body? Physical attributes? That's the world. Jesus said, "Sacrifice and offering you did not desire, but *a body* you have prepared for me." A beautiful body in the eyes of the Lord is one spent in self-giving, poured out as a libation in loving service, an instrument of self-donation. You have been gifted with a body fitted for that. In this light, your body is truly something beautiful for God, regardless of size, shape, and other dimensions. Like Jesus' body, it is meant to fulfill what is written in the book: "I have come to do your will, O God." In this spirit, Peter spoke to women:

> The affectation of an elaborate hairdress, the wearing of golden jewelry, or the donning of rich robes is not for you. Your adornment is rather the hidden character of the heart, expressed in the unfading beauty of a calm and gentle disposition. This is precious in God's eyes. (1 Peter 3:3-4)

Lord, the world is all green and gold
and blue outside,
and I'm all green and gold
and blue inside.

It's a day for the Magnificat.
I feel like a rainbow,

shot through with stars.
And it's all because
you love me
and I love you
and I know it!
It's because
you're here
and I'm here
and we're together.
Thank you, Lord, for days like this,
when your world and I sing
ALLELUIA!

SIXTH DAY—LUKE 6:20. "Blest are you poor; the reign of God is yours." Luke's redaction of the beatitude does not include "in spirit." You know it's not an oversight after you read Luke 12:13-21,22-32,33-34; 14:28-33; 16:9-13,14-15,19-31; 18:18-23,24-27; and 21:1-4. Luke, sometimes called the evangelist of Madison Avenue, is about as subtle as a sledgehammer when it comes to material poverty. He includes more of Jesus' sayings on the subject than the other synoptics or John. Why? What is Luke getting at here? Well, we could pose the question: Why does the whole world love Francis of Assisi, Mother Teresa of Calcutta, and Jean Vanier? Even unbelievers sense godliness and Christlikeness in those who believe so deeply in the Word that they act it out by literally becoming poor. How they come to resemble Jesus through complete trust in the heavenly Father! Even a disbelieving world says, "That's godliness!" It's exactly what Jesus said in Luke's version of the Sermon on the Mount: "Blest are you poor; the reign of God is yours." Jesus demonstrated a preferential love for poverty, obscurity, humility, and simplicity from His birth in swaddling clothes to His death on the cross when they cast lots for His clothes—the sign of a life lived in unconditional trust of the Father.

Not every Christian is given the call or the charism to heroic poverty; neither is any Christian excused from the gospel imperative of sharing his material resources with the poor (see James 2:15-17). John Woolman, a Quaker who died just before the American Revolution, wrote, "I found by experience that to *keep pace* with the gentle actions of Truth, and *never more but as that opens the way,* is necessary for the true servants of Christ." In the concrete circumstances of my life situation, what is the Lord Jesus Christ asking of me in the way of material poverty? Desiring neither more nor less than Truth requires, what gesture (big or little) shall I make today as a sign of my unconditional trust in the Father? The lofty principle of biblical poverty is realized on the pedestrian terrain of our daily experience.

Lord, do you always
have to answer me
when I talk to you?
Sometimes
I wish you wouldn't.
Today my monologue
was all cut out;
and then
you started
answering.

I complained to you
about the world
and the state
of its affairs.
And then you asked me
what I'd done
to change it.

I complained to you
about your church
and all the troubles
that beset it.
And then you asked me
what I'd done
to help it.

I complained to you
about the suffering
that I see:
the poverty, the illness,
the abuse of human rights.
And then you asked me
what I'd done
to alleviate it.

I complained to you
about some friends
who just didn't seem
to measure up
to what I had expected.
And then you asked me
what I'd done
to measure up
to them.

Lord, I'm beginning
to get the picture.
Stop complaining
and
start doing!

SEVENTH DAY—LUKE 9:49-50. It was John who said, "Master, we
saw a man using your name to expel demons, and we tried to stop

him because he is not of our company." Jesus told him in reply, "Do not stop him, for any man who is not against you is on your side!" A beautiful ecumenical gesture here. Anyone — regardless of denominational label or theological stance, whether self-righteous, theatrical, pompous, doctrinaire, tract-ridden, whether a fundamentalist or a Bible banger — who invokes the name of Jesus reverently is to be accepted as a brother or sister in the Lord. Cultural baggage notwithstanding, the person is saying, "I'm on your side." Ouch!

Lord, that conversation
a little while ago
didn't start out to be
a gossip session.
I don't know
what happened.
We started out
with a friendly chat
about ourselves
and our own problems.
And it was natural enough
to discuss those other people
we both know
and in whom
we are interested.
But somehow, Lord,
it got out of hand.
Suddenly I found myself
discussing
one of my sisters —
to her detriment.

At the time
I didn't stop to think

what I was saying.
And while the things
I said
were true,
that doesn't alter the fact
that they were unkind.
It doesn't alter the fact
that they need not
have been said at all.

I'm feeling guilty now,
and rightly so.
You would never have said
the things I said
of my sister.
I've damaged her image
in the eyes of another,
and how am I to restore it?

Lord, if there is a way
I can undo
the damage
I have done,
show me.
And, Lord, curb my tongue.
Teach me to speak
with charity
or not at all.

And Lord, forgive me.

EIGHTH DAY — JOHN 20:1-10. Early Sunday morning, as the sun begins to streak across the eastern sky — the stiff body — the chest begins to heave — a hand moves up slowly and uncovers

His face—He adjusts to the darkness—stands shakily—passes out of the tomb. Outside—He breathes the fresh air—He thrills to His new experience—He looks up to the hill and sees three empty crosses. He smiles and walks away.

This is my promise!

Lord, I want to sing,
I want to dance,
I want to celebrate!

I want to send up a skyful
of red balloons,
scatter the roads
with smiling daisies;
crash the cymbals,
beat the drums,
jangle tambourines,
clang the bells.

I want to shake the trees
and splash the fountains,
kiss the roses,
hug the world.

Lord!
Your love is like new wine.
I feel drunk with it!

About the Author

BRENNAN MANNING is a writer and speaker who leads spiritual retreats for people of all ages and backgrounds. He is the author of twelve books, including *Ruthless Trust*, *The Boy Who Cried Abba*, and *The Ragamuffin Gospel*. A resident of New Orleans, he travels extensively in the United States and abroad to share the Good News of the unconditional love of God.

More titles from Brennan Manning!

Abba's Child

Brennan Manning

978-1-57683-334-6

Author Brennan Manning encourages readers to let go of the stressful, unreal impostor lifestyle and freely accept our belovedness as children of God. Includes discussion questions.

The Rabbi's Heartbeat

Brennan Manning

978-1-57683-469-5

Brennan Manning brings us from a lukewarm, distant faith to being close enough to lean against Jesus, the Great Rabbi, and listen to His heartbeat. Adapted from his best-seller *Abba's Child*, this moving devotional is a daily reminder to soak in our Father's relentless love. As Abba's children, we need only to define ourselves through His Son just as the apostle John did: as one beloved by God.

Posers, Fakers, and Wannabes

Brennan Manning

978-1-57683-465-7

This book will help young people see how God's grace sets us free—free to be who we really are. No more games, no acts, no masks.

To order copies, call NavPress at 1-800-366-7788 or log on to www.navpress.com.